UNDER TH
MOON
A Story from the
Great War

Chris Durrant

A catalogue record for this book is available from the National Library of Australia

ACKNOWLEDGEMENTS

For general information about the war in East Africa I am indebted to Edward Paice whose well-researched and highly readable account of that little-known but bitterly fought sideshow of the Great War, *Tip and Run*, is surely the definitive work on the campaign. Thanks too to Tim Stapleton for his informative book *No Insignificant Part*, a history of the Rhodesia Native Regiment, and to Peter McLaughlin for his account of the Rhodesians in the War, *Ragtime Soldiers*.

I am most grateful to my dear (and very literate) friends Trea Wiltshire and Maureen de la Harpe for their wise advice and meticulous proof-reading. If there do remain any uncorrected grammatical or typographical errors, they are almost certainly due to my having unwittingly ignored their admonitions!

Finally, I must thank my wife Shirley for her support and for her indefatigable family research which really triggered the process that led me to write this story. At the end of the day, this book is probably her fault.

DEDICATION

To my uncle, Christopher Martin Durrant

Whose own story inspired this one

PROLOGUE

THE GRAVE

Mathew stumbled and almost fell as his foot caught on some unseen obstacle in the long dry grass that covered the path. Clearly it was some time since anyone had passed this way. The thorn trees stood like grey-green sentinels in the shimmering brown of the veldt. Not a breath of wind stirred their spiky foliage or relieved the heavy blanket of the mid-afternoon furnace. The only sound was the relentless continuum of the cicadas. Every other living thing appeared, very sensibly, to have retreated into some dark, cool, place to await the passing of the oppressive heat.

Except, of course, Mathew himself. The sweat trickled down his face and neck and stained the khaki cotton of his bush shirt, extravagantly purchased at the safari outfitters in Johannesburg. It also dripped onto his precious map as he stopped to estimate progress and he tried to flick the drops away before they could soak in and damage the paper. A futile exercise: the yellowish sheet, headed grandly 'Governo de Moçambique', was already stained and soggy. Still legible though. He looked up from the crude drawing of a little hill with rocks on top of it and there, just a few hundred metres ahead, was surely its real-life counterpart, a low stone kopje rising like an island from the tawny sea of the bush.

Mathew's arrival in Chokwe had caused a good deal of

excitement. Even now that the end of civil unrest had improved the security situation, very few foreign tourists ever passed through the town, and the appearance of this well-dressed white man in his shiny hired car with South African number plates had drawn a large crowd who cheerfully hung around the police station where Mathew checked in, and peered curiously through the windows of the vehicle at his exotic belongings within. The policemen were friendly and welcoming, and the letter of introduction from the Mozambique embassy in Pretoria evidently removed any suspicions there might have been as to Mathew's *bona fides*.

Unfortunately, none of the officers spoke English, and Mathew had barely a word of Portuguese beyond 'Ola' and 'Obrigado', let alone whichever African language it was that they spoke. However, whatever the embassy official in Pretoria had said in her letter (also, naturally, in Portuguese) and the loud repetition of certain key words (the word for 'cemetery', for example, is fortunately quite similar in English and Portuguese) were sufficient to establish Mathew's needs. When it came to directions, the sergeant in charge, a large, smiling man with an immaculately smart uniform and an almost overwhelming body odour, took control. On the official government note-pad he sketched a route northwards through the bush to the graveyard, writing what seemed to be the times against each section of the journey. He had then, by gestures at Mathew's watch and elaborate miming to indicate siesta, suggested that the journey be delayed until later in the afternoon when it would not be so hot. However Mathew was determined to press on, now that he was so close to his objective. He had no confidence in the sergeant's time estimates – surely the man was unlikely to have ever made the journey himself, or at least not in a motor vehicle – and the thought of being trapped in the bush by the sudden fall of the African night filled him with dread. With thanks and warm (very warm!) handshakes all round he had taken his leave and recovered his car from the rapt attentions of the curious mob. As he drove away, on an impulse he opened the window and scattered the barley sugars that he had bought in Maputo that morning. In the rear-view mirror he could see through the dust the raggedy urchins scrambling gleefully for the sweets.

As it turned out, the sergeant's estimates were surprisingly good. In little more than the predicted hour and a half Mathew had arrived at the banks of the dry donga where the track became impassable to vehicles and he had to abandon the Landcruiser. He was very loth to cast himself loose from his life-line to the outside world. The thought of having to make his way back on foot to civilization (if Chokwe could be so described) was appalling. However, the likelihood of people interfering with the car seemed very small. He had seen not the slightest sign of human life since leaving the main track an hour before. The worst that could happen, he decided, would be for him to return to the car to find it had been the subject of malicious damage by some large and destructive animal but in all honesty this did not seem likely either. A small antelope had scurried across the track in front of the car early on in the drive, and he had seen a few birds, but nothing of a size and disposition that would enable it inflict serious damage on one of the Toyota Motor Company's fine products. In any case, he evidently had no choice. Retrieving his camera and water-bottle, he made sure that he had thoroughly locked the car, trying every door in case the central locking mechanism was deceiving him. He then thrust the keys deep into his trouser pocket whence the chance of them falling out would be small, and set out along the path.

That had been about three quarters of an hour ago and now it seemed he was in sight of his goal. As he pushed along the path towards the hill, the fears that had always been lingering out of sight floated again to the surface. What if the gravestones had been destroyed or were indecipherable? What if the whole cemetery had been obliterated by the African bush? It was, after all, more than 90 years since the first broken bodies had been laid beneath the soil here, and probably not many fewer since the last burial. He had reason to believe that the graveyard had been maintained to some extent in colonial times, but those had ended more than 30 years ago. What if he had come all this way to find nothing?

Mathew need not have worried. The hill seemed bigger up close, and the boulders on its brow looked huge and black against the sky. The grass was thinner and it was easier to follow the path which led round the side of the kopje and towards a small cluster of thorn trees. As he looked eagerly ahead, a sudden flurry of activity from almost under his feet set his heart pumping and sent the sharp sting of adrenaline into his veins. Stepping back away from the commotion he tripped on some unseen obstruction and landed heavily and painfully on his backside. Heart still racing, he scrambled to his feet to face his assailant. Perched on the branch of a dead tree about ten feet in front of him was a large grey bird with a grotesquely huge yellow beak. The hornbill regarded him impassively for a few seconds with its beady black eye alongside that ludicrous beak, and then launched itself silently into the air and glided away out of sight behind the hill. It was the first living thing he had seen for nearly two hours.

Looking around, Mathew realized that he had arrived. Partly concealed behind the dead tree was a tall, stone cross embedded in a cairn of granite rocks. Cemented in the bottom of this was a metal plate. He had to reach down and rub the years of accumulated dirt and lichen off it to read the inscription MIGUBI HILL CEMETERY. He was in the middle of the graveyard.

Of most of the graves there was little or no remaining evidence. In some places a piece of whitened granite poked through the surface. In others there was nothing but a hump in the ground to suggest that any man-made edifice had stood there. The ones he had come to see, though, were in plain view, still standing together more or less erect. Obviously somebody had been looking after them: weeds had been removed since the growth of last rainy season, probably within the past few months. A small area beside the gravestones occupied by a large granite rock had also been cleared. As Mathew bent down to peer closer at the headstones, he could clearly read the inscriptions etched onto each. The date was the same for all of them – 4th March 1918. As he read them, Mathew had an extraordinary sensation of tunnel vision which cut out everything around him and focused on the three gravestones as his mind journeyed back across nearly a century to a time now almost beyond living memory, a world so different from today in almost every respect and yet one with which he felt a deep, compelling connection.

All of a sudden from nowhere came a powerful sense of grief and loss, so overwhelming that he fell to his knees. As he slumped there, camera and water-bottle forgotten on the ground beside him, he leaned forward until his forehead was resting against the warm, rough, granite of the middle headstone. He closed his eyes and tears coursed gently down his cheeks. It was the first time he had wept since he was a small child.

CHAPTER ONE

OLIVER

The pain in Captain Oliver Nayland's head had subsided to a dull ache. However, excessive movement was still inadvisable and he was more comfortable with his eyes closed. He had learned that this sort of hardship was part and parcel of the life of a soldier. On reflection, though, he had to acknowledge as a tactical error that last bottle of port the three of them had shared the night before. He lay very still on his back, propped up against the bed head, sipping the cup of tea that his batman, the disapproving Private Pyke, had brought him some ten minutes earlier. Oliver's mother was a firm believer in the restorative powers of tea, and it was a belief that Oliver wholeheartedly shared. Pyke, a rather dour, middle-aged Yorkshireman, had worked for him long enough to read the signs and provide the solution without having to be specifically instructed.

Movement, and the inevitable exacerbation of his pain, could, Oliver realized, no longer be delayed if he were to take full advantage of the two weeks' furlough he had been granted. One of his fellow officers, also going on leave and the possessor of a motor-car, had kindly offered him a lift to York, whence Oliver would be able to get a train home to Cowdenhall. This officer, who had prudently retreated from the mess the previous evening at least a couple of hours earlier than Oliver and his fellow-carousers, had said that he intended to be on his way soon after breakfast. So, draining the warm sweet dregs from his mug, Oliver swung his legs gingerly from the bed and stood up as slowly as he could to keep down the tide of pain and nausea. After a few seconds on his feet to stabilize his systems, he called in a hoarse voice for Pyke to bring the hot water and razor to prepare him for the rigours of the day.

Less than forty minutes later, sitting in the mess dining-room over a large bowl of porridge and a second steaming cup of well-sugared tea (he had not been able to face the eggs, bacon, sausages and kippers that smiled invitingly up at him from the silver dishes), Oliver was feeling a lot better. The prospect of a couple of hours in Lieutenant Radcliffe Fenchurch's jalopy was no longer quite so dreadful. That worthy sat opposite him, watching his superior officer eat with a sardonic but not unsympathetic smile on his lips.

"Well then, Ollie," he said at length, "are we under starter's orders?"

"Indeed we are, Fenchurch, indeed we are," replied Oliver through a mouthful of porridge. "Give me a few minutes to polish the fangs and get my kit, and we'll be on our way."

He was as good as his word and it was not long before he had taken his seat beside Fenchurch in the latter's elderly but reputedly reliable Napier 6-cylinder. Fenchurch's batman swung the crank-handle to bring the engine to life, and they were off.

The journey from Catterick to York was not a restful one. The Napier's fairly rigid suspension did little to minimize the roughness of the highway and it rained most of the time. Although well prepared with goggles, capes and mufflers, their defences were not complete, and both young men were drenched by the time the car chugged through the city walls and made its way to York railway station. Newspaper posters in the station yard blared WILL IT BE WAR? and the newsboys shouted, "France threatens Germany! Read all about it!"

"Do you think we'll get dragged in, Oliver?" said Fenchurch as he pulled up to allow his passenger to alight.

"I don't doubt it, laddie," said Oliver cheerfully as he rescued his kitbag from the back seat of the car. "The Kaiser's been spoiling for a fight for years, and it'll be up to us to give him a bloody nose. Don't worry, old boy !" He clapped his friend on the knee. "We won't miss out on the fun!"

As the train for Cowdenhall was not due to leave for an hour or so, Oliver made his way to the station buffet to fill in the gaps necessarily left by his inadequate breakfast. As with most forms of human activity, the process of recovery from hangovers is facilitated by frequent repetition. As he munched on the eggs and bacon which his revived constitution no longer rejected, he reflected on the prospect of war, the chances of at last putting all his training into practice. He had missed out by months on service in the South African war and, since then, had been stationed entirely in England and Ireland. His closest friend from school, Marcus Graythorpe, nearly a year his senior, had been posted to South Africa and had seen action in the dying stages of that bloody and vicious conflict between the Dutch farmers and the might of the British Empire. In fact Marcus was still in South Africa, having resigned from the army soon after the end of the war to pursue what he saw as the almost limitless business opportunities in that new and rapidly growing land. He and Oliver still corresponded regularly and, on his only visit home some years back, he had enthralled his friend with tales of courage and camaraderie out on the veldt, songs around the campfire in the evening, the adrenaline rush as Boer bullets fizzed through the air above your head, the satisfaction of a successful operation as the vanquished foe emerged, sullen and hard-eyed with their hands on their heads, from their hiding place in a farm-house.

Oliver's commanding officer, Colonel Henry Fortescue, was also a veteran of the South African war. A long, lean, leathery man, whose cynical disposition concealed a kind heart, the colonel had first fought in Africa during the Zulu wars when his extraordinary courage in saving the life of his commanding officer during a skirmish before the decisive battle of Ulundi had earned him the

Victoria Cross. He had also served with distinction under Lord Roberts in the more recent conflict, and had added the medal ribbon of the DSO to that of the VC. He had so far successfully resisted attempts to move him up the food chain into a staff position, preferring to remain embedded in the regimental environment that had been his home for more than 30 years. The colonel had never married and maintained a misogynistic exterior, although punctilious in his courtesy to those women with whom he was obliged to associate, such as the wives of his army colleagues. There had been a rumour, emanating who knows whence, that during the Boer war he'd enjoyed a liaison with the wife of a high-ranking South African official. Hard evidence of this, however, was not forthcoming and naturally none of his officers was game to raise the topic with the colonel himself.

Unsurprisingly, he was deeply respected by all the men under his command, and frankly worshipped by his junior officers, including even those of slightly more mature years such as Oliver. They listened spell-bound to his battle tales, drily factual and self-effacing though they invariably were. He shared Oliver's view of the inevitability of war with Germany, though not his enthusiasm for the prospect.

"War is a very nasty business," he had said, drawing on his post-prandial cheroot. "It does horrible things to men, and it makes men do horrible things. The best thing we as soldiers can do, gentlemen, is to be strong enough to prevent it happening and, if that doesn't work, to end it as quickly as we can." He had paused for a sip of port. "A modern war won't be like Waterloo or the Crimea – an away football game at someone else's ground. It'll affect everybody. Plenty of guts, gentlemen, but precious little glory."

Oliver, like most of the listeners, could dismiss the Old Man's pessimism as the cynicism of old age. His record, after all, spoke for itself. Oliver longed for the chance to put years of lessons into practice and even more to find out whether he truly had what it took to be a successful warrior. When the machine guns started to rattle, when the shells erupted around him and sent deadly shards of metal whirring about his head, would he still have the courage to go forward and engage the enemy, would he still be able think clearly and direct his men? Only the reality of battle would tell and Oliver could hardly wait.

Meanwhile there was the prospect of a pleasant and relaxing fortnight at home, away from the structured realities of army life at the barracks. He could exchange the gloomy and censorious ministrations of Private Pyke for the tender and loving care of his mother and sisters. He recalled that his elder sister Gertrude would be staying, together with her Canadian husband. It had been quite a few months since he had seen her. He was also looking forward to sharing fraternal banter with his young brother Humphrey, now apparently almost recovered from the savage bout of pneumonia which had so nearly claimed his life this winter.

And of course there was Mary. He grinned involuntarily at the thought of Mary Elizabeth Bath, his intended, with her soft blond hair, her eager blue eyes, and tremulous smile. His sister Molly, who had a sharp tongue, said that if she was any softer she would be a marshmallow. Gertrude, who was kinder, said she had a 'charming naivety'. Oliver's parents regarded her with a somewhat puzzled fondness. How had their feckless and fun-loving son managed to become engaged to such a sweet and guileless innocent? Oliver himself was happy to bask in her unconditional adoration, although a little voice deep inside sometimes queried the prospect of a lifetime with Mary. He never listened to this voice for long. She was, after all, very pretty and her father, who had inherited and augmented a fortune founded in the Lancashire cotton mills, was extremely rich. If his life needed additional spice, he reasoned, he could doubtless find it elsewhere.

With this agreeable and comforting thought, Oliver finished his meal, purchased his ticket and made his way to the train, where he settled into a window seat for the 45-minute journey to Cowdenhall. Perhaps, he thought, there might even be time for a nap.

§

After its brief and unhurried meander through the green and sodden Yorkshire countryside, the train at length pulled up, hissing gently, at the Cowdenhall station and Oliver alighted. Not having informed his family of his estimated time of arrival, he had not expected to be met, and it was a pleasant surprise to see the familiar figure of Humphrey standing there.

"Hallo, Piglet!" he said as they warmly shook hands. "Didn't think there'd be anyone here to meet me."

"Ah well," said Humphrey, taking possession of his brother's bag. "There were only three trains this afternoon and I need the exercise so I thought I might as well meet them all. Luckily for me you were on the first." The brothers walked companionably away from the station down the road towards the vicarage. Anyone seeing the two together would not doubt they were brothers – the same firm square jaw, the slightly beaky nose, the keen blue eyes. Humphrey, at 20 years of age, 12 years Oliver's junior, was a couple of inches below his brother's strapping six feet, and had inherited his mother's sandy hair rather than the dark brown that their father had bequeathed to Oliver. Humphrey's rather unfortunate nickname, now strictly only used *en famille*, was a relic of the days when, as a toddler, he had been in the habit of crawling about under the table, squeaking excitedly. He had, Oliver was glad to see, put on much of the weight he had lost during his recent illness. The previous autumn, on the point of going to Oxford to take up a place at Brasenose College, Humphrey had succumbed to a severe cold that had developed into full-blown pneumonia. For several weeks his life had hung in the balance and the family physician, fussy old Doctor Thwaites, had, on more than one occasion, advised his parents to prepare for the worst. However a naturally strong young constitution and the devoted attentions of his mother and sister Molly had confounded the doctor's fears and a few weeks before Christmas Humphrey was pronounced out of danger, though the struggle had left him pitifully emaciated and as weak as a baby. University had been indefinitely deferred and he had surrendered gladly to a process of rehabilitation based on good home cooking and tender loving care.

"Gertie here?" asked Oliver.

"Yes" replied his brother. "She and Mackenzie arrived on Monday". He grimaced slightly. "You'd better be careful, Ollie, she doesn't sign you up for the Empire".

"Good God! They're not still riding that horse, are they?"

"More than ever!" replied Humphrey. He assumed a mock Canadian accent. "Not only is it a moral imperative, it is your patriotic duty!"

Mackenzie Forrest, Gertrude's husband, several years her senior, was a Canadian who had made a substantial fortune in the lumber trade in his native Saskatchewan but now devoted much of his energies to the Empire of the Lord. This was a proselytizing Baptist church founded in Canada toward the end of the last century by the felicitously named Reverend Obadiah K. Jobsworth. Its main aim was to bring all the peoples of the British Empire together into one united church under the nominal leadership of the Reverend King Emperor (currently George V). Its members were vegetarians (all animals are God's creatures, and those who are intelligent enough to realize this should not feed on those who are not). A large section of the Empire also followed the example of some parts of the early Christian church in the use of cannabis as a means of facilitating communication with the Almighty. Mackenzie had fallen under the spell of the Reverend Jobsworth very soon after his marriage to Gertrude, and his wife had embraced the organization with even more enthusiasm than her spouse. Indeed, Oliver recalled, one of the reasons for their current presence in England, apart from visiting Gertrude's family, was to seek influential recruits to the cause in English society.

"How is father taking it?"

"Poor father!" said Humphrey with a laugh. "He is always polite, you know, but he keeps escaping to his study to prepare his sermon. I don't think I have ever known him take so much time to prepare a sermon. I hope it doesn't mean it'll be longer than usual." The Reverend Nayland's preaching, in the opinion of his younger children at least, tended to err on the side of prolixity.

"And mother?"

"She smiles and says 'Yes dear' and 'I agree dear' and 'I'm sure you're right dear' and then she slips out to the kitchen or the garden and it's left to Molly and me "

Oliver smiled and gave his brother an affectionate pat on the shoulder.

"And how do you handle it?"

"Well, Molly just laughs and says it's all complete tosh. They don't seem to take offence. I suppose they don't worry because she's just a girl. I have been saying that I can't think about important things while I'm still an invalid. I think that excuse is wearing a bit thin, though, now that I'm obviously as right as rain. It'll be good to have you, Ollie, as a diversion to draw some of the fire."

"We'll see about that! Anyway, Piglet, it's wonderful so see you looking so well – pretty much your old self."

They turned in at the vicarage gate and made their way up the gravel path to the front door. This opened before they got to it to release a small white yelping bundle of excitement which tore from one of them to the other, jumping up and rushing around in circles with sheer joy.

"Hallo, Dizzy," said Oliver, reaching down to pat the little dog, a rather unkempt Sealyham named, like all his litter mates, after a Victorian statesman, in his case Disraeli.

"Ollie!" Oliver felt his younger sister's arms locked around his neck, her soft brown hair against his cheek and breathed in her fresh smell, a combination of Palmolive soap and lavender water. He hugged her with genuine warmth.

"Let's look at you." She leaned back in his arms and scanned his face critically.

"You do look most distinguished – very military! Didn't shave very well this morning though." Her finger traced an unharvested patch of stubble below his jaw line.

"No, well, in a bit of a hurry! Hallo, Mother". He released Molly and stepped forward to exchange a warm embrace with his mother and a firm handshake with his father, who both stood beaming in the hall.

"It's so delightful to have you home, Oliver," said Mrs Nayland, putting her arm through his and drawing him close. "Gertrude and Mackenzie are in the garden. We thought it might be nice to have tea out there now that the rain has finished."

"Humphrey," said his father, "I wonder if I could beg a favour of you?"

"Of course," said Humphrey, putting Oliver's kitbag on the floor.

"I've got this little packet of books I promised to Albert Moffat last Sunday. I had meant to ask you before you went off to the station but I was too late. You know where his farm is, don't you?"

"I do," said Humphrey, taking the little parcel of books securely wrapped up with string. "I'll take my bike and it'll only be a few minutes. Don't let Ollie eat all the scones!"

§

The soft April light was filtering through the leaves of the large oak tree at the end of the lawn where the white cane outdoor furniture had been arranged for the comfort of the tea-drinkers. Fond greetings were exchanged, fresh scones and crumbly fruit cake consumed and tea (Indian or China, according to taste) sipped.

"How is the Empire, Mackenzie?" enquired Oliver, settling back to enjoy his fourth (or was it fifth?) cup of tea for the day.

"Slow progress, Oliver, slow progress," replied the Canadian. "Gertrude and I met some very pleasant folk in London who seemed to have a real interest in our cause. We have high hopes there."

"We were wondering," said Gertrude, "whether Mackenzie might be able to speak in your mess?"

"Oh, I don't think the colonel would countenance that," said Oliver firmly. "No disrespect, Mackenzie, but his view is that visitors to the mess, like little children, should be seen and not heard! Also, he doesn't want us taking our eyes off the ball. The defence of one Empire is going to be enough!"

"And how is Colonel Fortescue?" asked Louisa.

"Fighting fit, Mother!" replied Oliver, reaching forward to help himself to another scone.

"And what does he think about the possibility of war in Europe?"

"Oh, he is sure of it. We all are. It's just a matter of when."

"And does that not concern you?" enquired Mackenzie. "I read that the Germans and Austrians have more than a million men under arms, far more than we."

"Not at all," said Oliver firmly. "Numbers aren't everything. We have the finest, best-trained army in the world, the French have a huge force, and there is no doubt we'd have the Tsar with us too. No, the Kaiser is biting off more than he can chew this time, and we're going to give him a right royal bout of indigestion."

"I do hope you're right, dear," said his mother mildly, "though I must say I never really feel I can trust the French."

"I wonder where Humphrey is?" said Molly.

"He was kindly running a little errand for me," replied her father. "I would have expected him back by now. Perhaps his bicycle has sustained a puncture. Do make sure you leave him some scones, there's a good chap," he added in mild reproof to his elder son who was just demolishing his third one. "By the way, I forgot to mention, Oliver, that we have a letter for you from South Africa. Arrived last Saturday but we didn't send it on, knowing you'd be here soon. It's on my desk."

"Good-oh," said Oliver. "That'll be from Marcus."

"I'll get it for you," said Molly, springing out of her chair. She was back in a minute with the bulky blue envelope with its exotic stamps. "Come on, Ollie! Open it!"

He glanced around the circle of smiling faces before ripping open the envelope.

"He's fit and well," he reported after a moment. "He went big game hunting and shot a ... wildebeest – I think that's some sort of antelope." He read on for a minute. "Good gracious! He's joined the police!"

"Whatever happened to the camels?" wondered Aubrey. Marcus' most recent business venture, of which his previous letter had been full, had been the importing of camels from Arabia for use in South Africa's arid areas. It would, he wrote, revolutionise rural transport in the Union.

"He doesn't say. I'm guessing it didn't quite live up to expectations." This, sadly, was typical of Marcus' various and manifold business ventures over the years – a bright idea, a surge of optimism and enthusiasm, and, eventually, disillusion and failure.

"Actually," said Oliver after reading on a bit, "it seems that the force he has joined is not really police. It's called the British South Africa Police but it's more like a military unit. They are responsible for the defence of Rhodesia."

"Defence against what?" asked Gertrude.

"Oh, I don't know," said Oliver vaguely. "Savage natives? Rebellious Boers? Perhaps the Germans – they have several colonies in that part of Africa."

"Well, it all sounds very exciting," contributed Molly.

"He's got a message for you, Moll," said her brother with a smile. " He says he's saving for your *lobola*!"

"What's that?"

"Bride price, apparently!"

Everyone laughed and Molly coloured furiously. "What tosh!" she said. "I'm not going to marry anyone and, if I did, it certainly wouldn't be him!"

She was saved from further embarrassment by the entry of Humphrey.

"Sorry I'm late, Mother," he said, his face flushed, presumably with the exertion of cycling. "I got a bit diverted."

"Never mind, dear. We managed to save you some scones, but I fear the tea may be a little cold." Humphrey settled down and loaded up his plate and tea-cup.

"Oliver,"said his mother, "we have been invited to the Baths for dinner this evening. I am sure Mary Elizabeth is longing to see you."

"Good-oh!" said Oliver enthusiastically. "I can't wait to see her, too. What about a game of croquet, Piglet, before we have to get changed?"

"You're on!" replied his brother. "I must warn you, though, Ollie, to prepare to be thrashed. Molly and I have been doing a lot of practising since Christmas!"

§

Dinner at the Baths was a grand affair, at least in comparison to the simplicity of meals at the Vicarage. George Bath believed that his wealth gave him not only the opportunity but also the obligation to maintain certain standards. He was not a snob, but he did enjoy the good things in life. He and his wife Edith and their two children Mary Elizabeth and Hector lived in a fine late-Georgian residence, 'Beeches', in about 20 acres of grounds on the outskirts of Cowdenhall village. Albert did not consider that his duties as a pillar of the local community extended to the sharing of the inconveniences endured by most members of that community. One of his first actions on purchasing 'Beeches' some years before had been to install central heating, and his was the first house in the village to have a telephone and the first to be equipped with electric light in every room. He employed what Molly had once described as an "absurd number" of servants to keep the house and estate in apple-pie order, and these included an excellent cook. Consequently, even Molly and Gertrude, who instinctively disapproved of extravagance, secretly relished the occasions when they were invited to break bread at the Bath table.

This evening's meal, Oliver decided, had been well up to the usual standard, and he felt pleasantly full as he leant back in his chair and drew on one of his future father-in-law's excellent cigars. The ladies had retreated to the drawing-room, leaving the six gentlemen to their port or brandy (or mineral water, in the case of Mackenzie, who did not drink).

"Huntin' this Saturday, Oliver?" enquired Hector. "The meet's here."

Mary Elizabeth's brother was a large, somewhat untidy, young man, slightly pudgy, with a mop of fair hair.

"Love to!" replied Oliver. "Will I be able to borrow Hermes?"

"Of course. Mary's been exercising him to get ready for your visit." Oliver was a keen huntsman but did not own a horse, so had to rely on loans. This was yet another advantage of his liaison with Mary Elizabeth: the Baths had a large stable.

"What about you, Humphrey?"

His brother grimaced wryly.

"I'm not sure. Mother doesn't think I ought to. She says I mustn't over strain myself."

"Quite right," said his father firmly. "We don't want to undo all the good progress you've made."

"Oh well," said Hector, "if you are able to come, Pipkin is free and you're very welcome to him."

"Thanks, Hector," replied Humphrey. "I'll talk to mother. It is a special occasion, after all, with Ollie being here, and I've got to start leading a normal life eventually."

All the Nayland siblings were very competent riders and, when they were younger, it was not uncommon for all four of them to join the ranks of the Cowdenhall Hunt. Indeed, Molly had for several years owned her own pony, a sturdy little grey animal called 'Bread Sauce' or 'Saucy' for short, kept at a neighbour's farm. When she grew out of him, however, he was sold and not replaced and it seemed that Molly had lost some of her enthusiasm for fox-hunting. While she did not, perhaps, go quite as far as

Oscar Wilde's biting dismissal of the sport – 'the unspeakable in pursuit of the inedible' – she had evidently developed a great deal of sympathy with the fox, and although still relishing the excitement of the rustic gallops in the crisp morning air, Oliver suspected that she secretly rejoiced when the huntsman blew his horn to bring the hounds together after a fox had made its escape.

"Well, then, Oliver, when d'you reckon the Hun will attack?" asked George Bath, sipping at his cognac. The five years at Harrow that his father's wealth had obtained for him had almost, but not quite, eliminated his native accent. Occasionally, particularly in moments of stress, echoes of Cleethorpes could be detected.

"Hard to say, sir," replied Oliver thoughtfully. "They'd be mad to attack the French up front. I went over to France last year, you know, with a few other chaps from our corps on a jolly organized by the War Office. They have a huge army – we watched one of their exercises and their cavalry seemed to stretch forever. They have vast numbers of troops on the German border and lots of guns facing east. The French are still very bitter about the last little affray and I got the impression from their chaps that they are just longing for a chance to get their own back."

"What is to prevent the Germans simply going round the north of the French defences?" asked Mackenzie,

"Nothing, really," said Oliver with a short laugh, "but you would hope they will respect Belgian neutrality and, if they don't, we'll be there to stop them." The smoke from his cigar drifted lazily upwards and the flickering candles made the shadows dance on his lean, humorous, face. Mrs Bath refused to have the electric light on at dinner-time – "too harsh and garish, my dear, most unbecoming!" – so that the fine silver candle-sticks still had regular use.

"I read in the *Guardian*," said Aubrey, "that the Government thinks that the crisis has passed. Mr Churchill has organised a visit by the Navy to Germany this summer."

"I think that's more to gain a psychological advantage for the future than a gesture of friendship," said Oliver, taking a mouthful of his host's excellent brandy. "The Kaiser has been working up to this for years. Why do you think they've built such a massive navy?"

"Do you suppose," said his father, " that the army will need fresh volunteers if war breaks out?"

"Oh. I don't think so, father," said Oliver firmly. "The whole thing will be over by the winter. There wouldn't even be time to train them properly."

"Is that what your Colonel thinks?" asked Mackenzie.

"Well, no" said Oliver, smiling, "but he's a terrible old pessimist!"

"I'll tell you one thing," said Hector vehemently, his face slightly flushed with port and enthusiasm, "if the balloon goes up, I'll be volunteering straight away!"

"You'll do what is right" said his father firmly and somewhat ambiguously.

"Anyway," said Oliver, "let's forget about the Huns, what about the hunt this Saturday?"

"Well, we meet here as you know," said George, "and then I believe they are planning to make a start at the coverts by the lower wood on Rawlings' farm. Place is riddled with foxes, so he says, so they should be able to put one up without much difficulty."

"Good-oh!" said Oliver, "I can hardly wait!" He raised his brandy-glass on high. "Here's to good old Reynard! May he give us a run for our money!"

§

The day of the hunt dawned crisp and clear. There had been rain overnight, but by the time the riders all assembled on the drive and the circular lawn in front of the Bath's mansion, most of the clouds had cleared away, and the sunlight sparkled on the droplets of water on the grass and the leaves. It was cool, and Oliver was glad of the muffler round his neck as well as the kid riding gloves that had been a Christmas present from Mary Elizabeth. She herself was looking particularly gorgeous, her blond hair restrained by a hairnet beneath her riding cap, and her deep mauve riding skirt contrasting with the polished black of her riding boots. Her jacket, also black, was exquisitely cut to subtly hint at the perfection of the figure modestly concealed beneath it.

Around them all was subdued but excited chatter, as horses stamped and snorted, girths and clothing were given final adjustments, and spirits further heightened with the assistance of drinks carried round on silver salvers by Arnold the butler and Sykes the footman. The bright red jackets of the Master, Major Winter, and his assistants, provided a splendid splash of colour across the scene, and the hounds milled around the legs of the whipper-in, their tails waving in the air like so many bulrushes in the breeze.

At last it was time to move off, the huntsman sounded the call, and the pack, followed by the riders, moved slowly down the drive in the direction of Rawlings' farm, the gravel of the drive crunching crisply beneath the horses' hooves. Oliver waved to Molly who was standing with his mother and Mackenzie beside the lawn. Gertrude, looking very dashing in a black habit and cream riding skirt, was perched firmly on a large grey horse borrowed from the Bath stables. He looked in vain for Humphrey. Mrs Nayland had put her foot down on the question of her younger son joining the hunt that day, and Humphrey had acquiesced with surprising meekness. Oliver remembered his brother had brought his bicycle with him and decided that he must have gone off to find a good vantage point from which to watch proceedings. It wasn't long before the hounds put up a fox near Rawlings' wood, and Oliver's pulse quickened as the huntsman sounded 'gone away' and the pack streamed up the field, followed by the riders, many cheering enthusiastically. Oliver caught a glimpse of a small red shape in front of them all, darting through the hedge at the top of the meadow, and before long he was setting his horse at the same hedge and the massive, snorting Hermes hauled his muscular bulk effortlessly over to land with a jolt in the grass on the other side.

Out of the corner of his eye, Oliver could see that Mary Elizabeth and her mount had also successfully negotiated the first fence and were thundering along at his shoulder. The fox, meanwhile, had evidently decided that running away from the woods was a tactical error and, once through the fence, had doubled back along it down the hill again towards the cover. The hounds were momentarily confused, but it wasn't long before they picked up the scent and the pack set off again with the riders in hot pursuit.

The next fence was a slightly awkward one on the crest of a low bank and, as he and Hermes soared over, Oliver saw that the meadow on the other side was quite a bit lower than the one they had just taken off from. They landed with an even greater jolt and Oliver almost lost his seat, but Hermes, strong and sure-footed, soon regained his poise and they cantered on without mishap. Mary Elizabeth was not so lucky. Oliver heard a cry and, reining in his mount to look around, saw his fiancée, hatless, sitting on a horse that had slowed to a stumbling walk. Swiftly he turned and cantered back.

"Are you alright, darling?"

"I'm fine, Oliver. We just landed awkwardly and I nearly came off but managed to hang on." Her face was flushed with excitement and some wisps of blond hair had escaped from the net.

"But I think Pandora has gone lame. She must have twisted her leg as we came down."

Oliver jumped to the ground and, holding Hermes' reins, first retrieved Mary Elizabeth's riding hat and then bent down to examine her horse's near front leg which the animal was evidently avoiding putting much weight on. Carefully he felt his way along the fetlock, while Pandora stood patiently, just uttering a gentle whinny when he pressed on what must have been a tender spot.

"I don't think it's too serious," he said at length. "I think, as you say, she's given it a twist. We'll have to go back though. She can't go on." Oliver could feel the disappointment bitter in his throat. He had been greatly looking forward to this morning.

"Oh no, Oliver, I'll be alright. You don't have to come back with me."

"Are you sure? I think I ought to. What will your father say?"

"I'll be fine, honestly. The road is just over there and once we're on that I'll walk her back. Don't worry about Daddy. I'll tell him I insisted! "

Oliver felt a resurgence of joy within him.

"Well, if you're quite certain….?"

"I am. You go and enjoy yourself and I'll see you at home for lunch." Mary Elizabeth blew Oliver a kiss and turned Pandora's head towards the big gate at the side of the field that led to the nearby road. Oliver checked Hermes' girth to ensure that the jolting had not loosened it and then swung himself back into the saddle. He watched while Mary Elizabeth reached the gate where she dismounted and led Pandora through before turning and giving him a final wave. Oliver reflected on how lucky he was to have such an understanding girl. He didn't envy her the walk home. A mile over country roads in riding boots was going to leave her very sore. Still, he would make it up to her. No pain that a little tête á tête in the Bath's summer house would not dissipate!

While all this drama had been occurring, the hunt had disappeared from view. Oliver could hear, very distantly, the sound of the horn which told him that the chase was still in progress. It sounded as though, after returning to the wood, they had turned off down the valley close to the little brook that ran there. That being so, he reasoned, he would more readily catch up with the action if he took to the road, which cut directly across the hill-side before intersecting the brook at Ballard's Bridge. It wasn't long before he too was jogging along the cobbled surface, travelling in the opposite direction to that taken by Mary Elizabeth and the hapless Pandora. He hadn't gone very far before he saw a disembodied head appearing above the hedges that lined the road, coming towards him at pace. As it got nearer and the body came into view, he was surprised to recognise Humphrey, hatless and dishevelled, pedalling furiously along on his bicycle.

"Ollie! Thank goodness it's you! Come quickly! Gertie's had a fall!"

§

The brothers dismounted at a gate leading into a long field that stretched down the hill. Oliver tied Hermes' reins to the gate post and Humphrey left his bicycle on the ground as they ran down through the lush grass. Oliver could see two figures sitting beneath a tree at the bottom of the meadow with a grey horse, presumably Gertrude's, standing nearby.

"Who's that with her?" Oliver asked.

"Ruth," said Humphrey. " I left her looking after Gertie while I rode for help."

"Ruth who?"

Humphrey didn't reply but ran on and soon they arrived at the tree. Gertie was sitting with her back against it, her face white as chalk but her eyes open and the ghost of a wry smile on her lips. The woman next to her was kneeling on the ground, holding Gertrude's hand in both of her own. She looked up smiling as the men approached.

"Hello, Humphrey," she said. "She woke up just after you'd gone, so we moved against the tree and I've tied up her horse. He seems to be alright."

"Well done, Ruth," said Humphrey warmly."Are you fit, Gertie? I thought you were dead for a minute."

"I'll live" said his sister faintly, "though I've got a fearsome headache and my shoulder is agony. Your friend has been so kind."

"Yes – Ollie, Gertie, this is Ruth, Ruth Moffat. Ruth, this is my brother and sister."

"Pleased to meet you" said Ruth extending her hand to shake Oliver's. She was, he saw, little more than a girl but with a calm, self-possessed air about her. Her hand when he shook it was small and firm. Her face was tanned with a sprinkle of freckles on the cheekbones and her brown hair tied back with a plain green ribbon, fell behind her shoulders. Her eyes, which looked directly into his without a trace of embarrassment or unease, were an unusual grey.

It was, he reflected, one of the most pleasing faces he had ever seen.

"We need to get you home, Gertie," said Oliver, " and have old Thwaites round to take a look at you. I bet you've dished your collarbone." Oliver was something of an authority on minor fractures, having accumulated an impressive record of them himself during an incident-filled childhood.

"We could take her to our farm first," suggested Ruth. "It's much closer." Her voice was low and melodic, with the broadening of the vowels natural to the inhabitants of the East Riding of Yorkshire.

"Good idea," said Oliver. "Come on, Gertie. Let's see if we can get you up on your nag."

§

Some time later, after a rather slow and painful progress along the country lanes to the Moffat farm, they were all gathered in the warmth of the parlour, Gertrude comfortably stretched out on a settle while Ruth, and a young girl who had been introduced as her sister Emily, bustled about organising cups of tea for all and cushions and a blanket for the invalid. Humphrey had pedalled off to get help while Oliver had tied both horses up in a cowshed next to the house, having made sure that there was hay and water for them. He had to duck his head to enter the farmhouse, and accepted a steaming cup of tea from Emily who seemed rather shy and flushed when he thanked her. She was very like her sister to look at, though with blue eyes rather than grey, and lacking the air of calm serenity that Ruth possessed.

Over the rim of his teacup, Oliver watched the elder girl as she went about her tasks, refilling the kettle and placing it on the stove, checking Gertrude's comfort, and stoking up the stove with some coal from a hob beside it. She was below middle height, and her plain cotton dress and pinny concealed a trim figure supported by slender ankles and small feet. She was, he decided, an absolute pippin. How, he wondered, had Humphrey discovered her? For the first time in his life he felt a tiny twinge of jealousy towards his brother.

"Your father is out somewhere?" he asked.

"Aye" she replied, "he's up at the bitings on the fell. We've three ewes due to lamb and he went to mind them. I'd be with him but … well, I were watching the hunt." For the first time she seemed a bit awkward. "Any road, he'll be back for his dinner before too long."

In the event, Farmer Moffat's return almost coincided with the arrival of the Bath automobile, driven by George Bath himself with an anxious Mackenzie on the front passenger seat and Humphrey in the back. Albert Moffat was a man of stocky build and middle height, with keen blue eyes that regarded the world rather sternly from a face lined and tanned by a lifetime of hard work in all weathers. An old stiff-brimmed hat was pulled down firmly over his brow and grizzled sideburns framed the same determined jaw as his daughters. Greetings were exchanged (Albert knew all present except for Mackenzie) and explanations made while the two Moffat dogs also busily investigated the situation, sniffing around legs and car wheels until brought to heel by a sharp word from their master. All then went inside to gather sympathetically around the invalid, still stretched out on the settle.

§

That evening the family assembled round Gertrude's bed-side. Dr Thwaites, beaky, bespectacled, and stern but not without a somewhat lugubrious sense of humour, had been round and confirmed Oliver's diagnosis of a broken collar-bone. Other than this, even his inbuilt medical pessimism had been unable to find anything but a mild concussion. Gertrude's arm had been firmly strapped and immobilised in a sling and she had been strictly adjured to remain in bed for at least a week, and refrain from any serious physical exercise for two months. "Yours is the third broken limb I've had to patch up today," he said as he packed up his bag." "It's quite beyond me why you people insist on hunting. But if you must, could you learn not to fall off your horses?"And with that he had made his farewells and let himself out.

"I'm afraid I'm not going to be much use to the campaign for a while," said Gertrude, smiling up at her husband. She was still quite pale as she sat propped up in bed against a mountain of pillows.

"My dear, do not concern yourself with that," said Mackenzie earnestly, squeezing her free hand with both of his. "Your health is far more important. We'll manage."

"What I want to know," said Oliver, perched companionably on the end of his sister's bed, "is where young Piglet has been keeping this paramour of his?"

"What do you mean?" said his mother.

"Ruth!" said Oliver, smiling wolfishly, "the lovely Ruth!"

"She helped after the accident," explained Gertrude. "She was so kind. She's Farmer Moffat's daughter."

"She's not a paramour!" said Humphrey indignantly, colouring fiercely, "I met her when I took those books round for Pa. We just agreed to watch the hunt go by."

"She's in church on Sundays with Albert," said his father, "she and her younger sister. Seems a nice lass. She's just a young girl."

"She's eighteen!" said Humphrey.

"Aha!" said Oliver triumphantly. "Been doing some intimate research, Piglet!"

"Don't be mean, Oliver," said Molly crossly. "You shouldn't assume that everyone has your barrack-room attitudes."

"We shall see," replied Oliver with mock gravity. "I detect romance! Mark my words, my friends, mark my words!"

CHAPTER TWO

HUMPHREY

Life had never seemed very complicated to Humphrey. His place in the great scheme of things was well defined and assured and he was perfectly happy with it. Safe within the cocoon of his close and loving family, little had happened so far to shake his confidence in the system of which he was a part. The one tragedy to affect his immediate family, the death of his older brother Archie from whooping cough, complicated by pneumonia, had occurred a year or two before he was born.

Boarding school at the age of thirteen had, in a way, quite changed the tenor of his existence but this was part of the context within which he was brought up and he had to some extent experienced it vicariously through Oliver. His brother was, of course, long gone by the time Humphrey got to St Peter's York, but his reputation lived on and served to cushion Humphrey's entry into what could be a harsh and hostile environment.

Even his own illness, which at one point had seemed likely to send him to join Archie in the little parish graveyard behind the church, had done little to undermine his faith in the integrity of his society. At the height of the crisis he was just enveloped in a fevered misty, painful cloud, barely aware of where he was. Once he returned to consciousness, he found himself ensconced in familiar surroundings, cradled by the love and care of Molly and his mother, with the benevolent but rather worried visage of his father floating occasionally into view in the background.

His meeting with Ruth, however, was quite another matter, and an experience for which he was completely unprepared. He knew about girls, naturally, and had watched with the same often censorious amusement as the rest of the family Oliver's escapades with the fair sex over the years. His personal interactions with females outside his immediate family were confined to a few dances in the village hall and a memorable Valentine's Day ball at the Baths' house where he had his first kiss, a trembling, hurried, and curiously unsatisfactory encounter on the terrace in the moonlight which had left both participants exhilarated but slightly horrified. The girl, a distant cousin of the Baths, was whisked away by her parents after the ball, and he had never seen nor heard from her again. The only other female close to his own age with whom he had any intimate relationship at all was Molly and she was, after all, a sibling, friend and playmate, and only incidentally a woman.

When he was, unexpectedly, confronted by Ruth after he had knocked at the farm house door, he was momentarily speechless. The girl smiled at his confusion.

"Hallo" she said, "can I help you?"

"Er, yes, I've got something for Farmer Moffat, from the Vicar."

"Oh. Well he's out at the moment but you can leave it here." As he stood uncertainly on the doorstep she took pity on him.

"Come in," she said.

Humphrey followed her into the hallway which led directly into the kitchen. A solid wooden table stood in the middle with several chairs around it. Against the left wall was a large cooking range and oven that accounted for the warmth of the room and a wide window looking out over what appeared to be a vegetable garden with a lush green meadow beyond. A large black and white cat lay curled up on the floor by the stove. It did not stir as they came in.

"Sit you down," Ruth said, indicating one of the chairs by the table. "I must just finish this or the bread'll end up sad." She was kneading a large knob of dough on the table and her hands were white with flour.

"Dad'll be back directly. I'm Ruth."

"Oh! And I'm Humphrey."

"I know. The Vicar's lad." She smiled at his surprise. "I've seen you in church. I dare say you won't recall, but we went to Sunday School together when we were bairns."

"I'm sorry," said Humphrey."I don't remember."

"It were a good time since, and I were a couple of years younger than you."

Humphrey watched as the girl put the dough into two baking tins which she set to rise near the stove. She was slim and upright, her long brown hair tied back out of the way with a black ribbon, though one wisp had escaped to hang over her face which no doubt accounted for the smudge of flour on her cheek. Her face was gravely concentrated as she went about her business with the bread but lit up with a smile when she glanced in his direction. She was the most beautiful creature he had ever seen. How could he possibly not remember her? Abruptly he recalled his mission.

"I've got these books for your father."

"Aye, just leave them on the table. Dad's so grateful for the books from the Vicar. He really enjoys them. So do I."

"Do you read them as well?"

"Sometimes. I will say I'm not that smitten with the Roman poets, but I do love the history. Would you like a cuppa?"

"Oh, yes .. thanks." Anything to prolong his stay.

The tea was very hot and very strong. Ruth rinsed her hands in the sink and dried them on her apron. She sat opposite him at the table. They talked. He learned that her mother had died five years before in the diphtheria outbreak and she now kept house for her father and her younger sister Emily. She knew all about his illness.

"We prayed for you in church, you know. Your dad were that worried. God must have listened!"

Mention of his family roused Humphrey into remembrance of where he was supposed to be. Getting to his feet he thanked Ruth for the tea.

"Will I see you again?" he blurted.

The girl looked steadily into his face. "I hope so," she said.

As he clambered onto his bike and pedaled off down the lane, Humphrey's heart was racing and his mind was dancing with delight.

§

Humphrey got his chance to renew his acquaintanceship with Ruth rather earlier than he might have expected. His mother had firmly vetoed his participation in the hunt and for once he had meekly acquiesced. He timed his return to the farm for when he judged Emily was likely to be at school and her father out and about his business on the farm. His judgement was good. Neither was in evidence. Ruth did not answer his knock on the door but soon emerged from the barn where she had been collecting eggs.

"The hunt's meeting at the Bath's place this Saturday," said Humphrey after they had exchanged shy greetings. "I can't ride this week, but I was going to go around and watch as much of the fun as I could. I wondered if you'd like … er … if you'd be able to come with me?"

"I'd love to," replied Ruth without hesitation and Humphrey's heart leapt with joy again.

They arranged to meet at the end of the lane leading to the farm and, on the day of the hunt, set off from there, Humphrey pushing his bike. Walking beside her through the cool, fresh, beauty of a country morning was exhilarating and Humphrey felt quite intoxicated. The lanes and woodland they passed through were alive with a variety of birds which Ruth was able to identify. They watched as a pair of hedge sparrows foraged in the ditch and laughed at the quarrelsome chattering of a group of goldfinches. Ruth showed him the scraping at the bottom of the hedgerow which was a thoroughfare for a badger's nocturnal ramblings.

"There's a sett in the spinney by the farmhouse ley," she said. "Emily and I have sometimes crept there on a moonlit night and watched them come and go." She smiled. "Dad's not best pleased. He reckons they come for the chicks and the eggs."

"And do they?"

"Aye, mebbe. But if we close the barn doors at night there's no harm done."

It was fortuitous that they were overlooking the bank over which Gertrude and her mount came to grief, and were able to rush down to her aid. Humphrey was amazed at the way Ruth calmly took control of the situation, helping him to carry his sister to shelter where she made her comfortable while Humphrey caught the horse. She then sent him off on his bike to fetch help while she elected to stay with the still unconscious woman.

§

The Gertie incident in many ways precipitated Ruth and Humphrey's relationship. Perceptive observers, such as Molly and young Emily, were soon in no doubt that this was more than just a casual acquaintance. Humphrey became a regular visitor at the Moffat farmhouse, though, for propriety's sake, he tried to confine his visits to times when either her sister or her father were present. When she had spare time from her house-wifely duties they would walk for miles through the woods and byways around the village.

Humphrey was surprised at how articulate Ruth was. Her schooling had been abruptly terminated at 13 when her mother died, but she was very well read and evidently had an enquiring mind. She was able to open to him the treasure chest of her familiarity with the countryside and, for his part, he was able to broaden her vision of the world outside Cowdenhall of which his knowledge, although far from extensive, was considerably wider than hers.

He could remember with great clarity their first kiss. They were seated on a fallen log looking down the valley. She had glanced up at him and, on an impulse he had bent down and kissed her lightly on the lips. For two seconds she gazed at him wide-eyed. Then she reached up with her hand and drew his face down again to hers. After a while they parted and sat in breathless silence. Ruth took Humphrey's hand in both of hers and seemed to examine it carefully.

"I've never had a sweetheart," she said.

"I've never kissed a girl, not properly." The Valentine's night episode on the Bath terrace was dismissed in his mind as an irrelevancy. He gazed at her as she sat beside him, cheek slightly flushed, eyes downcast. The usual errant wisp of hair had escaped from its ribbon. He reached to brush it away and when she turned to him with a smile he leaned over and kissed her again. Her soft warmth, her fragrance, the touch of her hands on his back, filled his senses. In a while they got up by mutual impulse and walked on, hand in hand, until they came within sight of the farmhouse when a more seemly separation was resumed.

§

It had been a very wet start to the English spring and March had seen rainfall records set in many parts of the country. However, it seemed that the alignment of Ruth and Humphrey's stars had turned off the tap and the countryside basked in the most glorious weather that anyone could remember. Dewy fresh mornings merged into mild sunny afternoons that promised a sweltering summer to come. This made it much easier than it might have been for the pair to meet away from the scrutiny of their families. Humphrey had no particular regular duties or responsibilities and when Ruth was able to get away from hers they would go off on long rambling walks through the woods and down the dales around the Moffat farm. They often met people on their way, usually villagers or farm folk going about their business, who would greet them cheerfully. "Nah then, Ruthie, morning, master Nayland." Once they encountered a strange man who stepped into a glade where they had stopped. He gave them a shock when he appeared from behind a bush, a wild-eyed man with long matted hair and a raggedy beard. His clothes were worn and patched and looked none too clean and he was carrying an old battered valise. Ruth gripped Humphrey's hand tightly as the stranger and the couple stared at each other wordlessly. He then nodded at them before brushing past and disappeared down the path. Ruth and Humphrey gazed at each other in amazement for a few seconds before bursting out laughing.

They talked endlessly, each eager to find out all there was to know about the other. Humphrey told her about his school days (the choir, the cricket 2nd XI), the feverish nightmare of his recent illness, and the devoted nursing from his mother and sister.

"Ma says that if it hadn't been for Molly she doesn't think I'd have come through."

"Then I owe her a big debt," said Ruth, rubbing her cheek against his shoulder. She had painful memories of her mother's fatal illness five years before. Her aunt, who lived in York, had come to help nurse her but the disease took a swift course and Elizabeth Moffat was dead soon after her sister arrived.

"Dad took it very hard," said Ruth. "Mum were the joy in his life. Whenever he got too grumpy she'd laugh him out of it. There's nobody to do that now, so he's grumpy a lot."

Grumpy certainly seemed to Humphrey a fair description of Albert Moffat. When they met, over a cup of tea around the farm kitchen table, the farmer's demeanour was grim and unforthcoming, his conversation, though polite, tended to be monosyllabic. He would usually excuse himself at the earliest opportunity to go off and resume his chores. Emily, on the other hand, was the very antithesis of grumpy. A lightweight, more frivolous version of her elder sister – a water colour to Ruth's oil painting – she flirted outrageously with Humphrey and would pout petulantly when Ruth found her some essential duty to divert her.

Humphrey's own family was similarly ambivalent. Gertrude's accident had ensured that there was no chance of keeping Ruth a secret from them, although it was a little while before he brought her round to meet his parents. This event, the customary tea and scones in the garden, was somewhat awkward. Ruth, overawed by the occasion, was most uncharacteristically reticent, which led to Louisa remarking to her son afterwards, "Seems a nice girl, Humphrey, but she doesn't say much."

"Get's that from her father, I don't doubt," said Reverend Nayland with a chuckle, but he too wondered at the attraction of this mousy little thing for his son. From his sisters, Humphrey had almost unqualified support. Gertrude, who had been forced to change her plans and stay on longer at the vicarage to recover from her fall, had seen Ruth in action and remained deeply grateful to her. Molly knew Humphrey better than anyone and could instantly see that Ruth was important to him, at least for the time being.

"Be careful, Piglet," she said, with a wisdom beyond her years. "It's so easy to hurt people, even if you don't mean to."

"I'd never hurt Ruth!" he replied indignantly.

"I know," she said, placing her hand on his arm. "Just be careful."

CHAPTER THREE

RUTH

Growing up on a farm shapes a person in many ways. You tend not to develop the habit of dreamy introspection: there is always something that needs doing. Even children are expected to do what they can – collecting eggs, carrying water from the pump, bringing the cattle in from the meadow for milking. In Ruth's case this process was reinforced by her mother's premature death which had thrust upon her adult duties and responsibilities when she was still just a child.

Despite this, being, unlike most girls of her class, not only literate but with a love of literature which led to her to spend much of what little spare time she did have reading, Ruth had a knowledge of ideas and events outside her own experience that was unusual. Her mind could, and did, play with ideas beyond the barnyard. She did not, of course, have an opportunity to discuss these ideas with anyone else. None of her village friends would have understood her, and her father was not one to indulge in philosophical chit-chat, as he would no doubt have put it.

Another defining influence of farm life was a knowledge, absorbed from an early age, of what polite society might have termed 'the facts of life'. No-one who had seen the ram having his wicked way with the ewes, or watched, as Ruth had, while her father helped to ensure that the boar's amorous advances to his sow were not misplaced, could have remained ignorant of how things worked. On a farm, as a later song would have it, love was all around you. Had she harboured any doubts that this sort of behaviour applied equally to the human animal, they would have been dispelled at the age of six when, woken in the night by noise from her parents' room, she had padded next door in her night-shirt to discover her parents engaged in what the Victorian novelists she later read so avidly might have described as 'a mutual exchange of affection'. Appalled and fascinated, she watched for a minute from the doorway until her presence was noted and she was sent firmly, but not unkindly, back to the bed she shared with Emily.

As she grew into puberty, Ruth had felt within herself the stirring of primal longings that could not entirely be sublimated by the domestic drudgery that was her lot. Her entry into puberty had coincided with her unexpected assumption of the role of housewife and her consequent withdrawal to a great extent from the daily company of her peers reduced her opportunities for dalliance. Despite this there had been several episodes of teenage groping, none of which ended satisfactorily for either party. When she told Humphrey she had never had a sweetheart, this was the truth. Ruth had felt a conflict between her inner urgings and the ideals absorbed from her reading about the relationship between a man and a woman. The resultant stand-offishness had not endeared her to the local lads, one of whom had told her that she was a stuck-up cow.

Meeting Humphrey had seemed to give her the chance to satisfy these two previously conflicting needs. For the first time she felt she could let her emotions off the leash. She had been aware of Humphrey for some years: she saw him in church most Sundays, and on visits to the village she had occasionally seen him pedaling along on his bike. She had always been attracted to his calm demeanour, his usual gravity often enlivened by mischief and laughter as he shared a joke with Molly. At that first encounter, when she had seen him above the hatch, standing there on the doorstep clutching the little packet of books, his face slightly flushed with embarrassment, her heart had gone out to him. Really from that moment she was lost. Over the years she had unconsciously imbued him with the character traits she most admired in a boy and, as she got to know him better, she discovered that, by and large, he fitted the mould she had made for him. She remembered old Mrs Waggoner, who often did cleaning jobs up at the vicarage, saying to her father, "That Master Humphrey, he don't have an unkind bone in his body". And it was true. If he did make a critical comment about anyone, it was always leavened by a sympathetic caveat.

For virtually the first time she found someone her own age who was prepared to listen to her, who thought that her opinions were valuable. They talked endlessly on a wide range of topics and, if it was one of the many subjects about which he was better informed than she, there was never a trace of arrogance or superiority. She respected the affection and loyalty he had for his family, which she could understand, and for his old school, which she could not. She thought some of his character judgements naïve but found that more attractive than the pervading cynicism she often found in others. Underneath the gentle exterior she sensed a firmness and courage that she also warmed to. In their little confrontation with the wild man in the woods, his first reaction had been to grip her hand firmly and take half a step forward as though to interpose himself between her and a perceived threat.

As for the chemistry between them, it was clear from the start that he felt much as she did. There was initially a somewhat uncomfortable tension between them, relieved to a great extent by that first kiss and the subsequent greater physical intimacy. In their embrace she could feel the urgency of his need but he was always restrained and never tried to take advantage of her feelings. Once, when his hand brushed inadvertently against her breast, he had immediately apologized. Her first impulse had been to seize the offending hand and press it against the part of her where it had unwittingly strayed, but instead she had laughed and hugged his arm and said, "It don't matter, Humphrey."

Like it or not, she shared his view of pre-marital sex – it was against God's law. Her unquestioning respect for the Almighty had been more than little shaken by the arbitrary and unjust event of her mother's death. How could a benevolent and omnipotent deity snatch away such a beautiful person, causing hardship and grief for those left behind? However, a lessened confidence in the ruler did not immediately translate into a lack of respect for the rules. This placed a sharp focus on the future of her relationship with Humphrey. Could they simply continue as they were? (Surely not) How could it progress to a new level?

Ruth knew that it was not at all uncommon for girls her age to get married. For Humphrey, though, it would be quite another matter. He had no career, no occupation, no commercially useful skills. Even with the unstinting support of both their families, which she had a shrewd suspicion would not be forthcoming, there would be huge practical difficulties.

They often talked about Humphrey's immediate future.

"I suppose I'll be going up to Oxford in the autumn," he said, without great enthusiasm.

"That'll be wonderful! What will you be studying?"

"Well, I was down to read Classics – your favourite Roman poets, that sort of thing. But I'm not so sure I want to go now."

"Don't be daft, Humphrey! You'll have a wonderful time! Think of all the things you'll learn and all the interesting folk you'll meet."

He looked at her and gently traced the sweet line of her jaw with his fingers.

"I don't want to meet interesting folk, Ruthie. I want to be with you."

She sighed and gave herself up to a long and satisfying kiss.

§

Some form of confrontation with her family was inevitable and was in fact not long coming. Albert Moffat was seated at the table having his tea. It had been a long day. Two of his sheep had strayed off his property, possibly chased by dogs, and he had searched for a couple of hours before finding them, huddled in the lee of a dry-stone wall on a neighbour's field some way away.

"What's up wi' you and the Vicar's lad?" he asked Ruth as she took his plate away to wash it.

"Nowt," she replied, turning to the sink to conceal what she knew must be a tell-tale blush. "I've just met up with him a couple of times."

"Ruthie's sweet on Humphrey!" chanted Emily gleefully.

"I am not!" said Ruth indignantly.

"Are too!" retorted her sister. "I've seen the way you look on him."

"Any road," interposed their father, "I don't want you thinking about that sort of thing, Ruth. He's a decent young feller, but he's nobbut a lad and soon he'll be off to the university and you'll be biding here." He got to his feet. "Think on, lass, think on."

Ruth did think on.

Coincidentally, it was not long after this that she formally met Humphrey's parents for the first time. Louisa had suggested to Humphrey that he might like to bring Ruth round for a cup of afternoon tea, and when Humphrey explained that that time of day did not fit in very well with Ruth's duties around the home – being there when Emily returned from school, and making the family's evening meal – the occasion was changed to morning tea. To say that Ruth felt apprehensive about it was putting it mildly. She had of course met the Vicar and his wife often at church and exchanged polite pleasantries, but these circumstances were very different.

The effort of trying to say the right thing (whatever that might be), managing the saucer, tea-spoon and other unfamiliar impedimenta of polite middle-class society, and trying to create a favourable impression on Humphrey's parents placed a considerable strain on Ruth and eroded her usual self-confidence. She was thankful for the fact that Gertrude was not there – her collar-bone had evidently mended remarkably well and she and

Mackenzie had left for London two days previously – and the Vicar excused himself fairly early and retreated to his study so she was left with Mrs Nayland and Molly. Humphrey had been firmly told by his mother that his presence was not required.

"How is your young sister getting on at school?" asked Louisa as she poured herself another cup of tea. Ruth's first cup stood almost untouched.

"Oh. Well, ma'am," said Ruth. "She's that sharp. She says she wants to be a schoolmistress."

"And what about you, Ruth?" asked Molly. "What do you want?" Ruth felt instinctively that Molly was on her side, though she could not help but feel a twinge of jealousy at the easy intimacy the young woman evidently had with her brother.

"I don't know," she replied. "I suppose I'll bide at home and mind Dad while he needs me."

"That's all very well," said Molly firmly, "but you've got your own life to lead."

Ruth said nothing and sipped her, by now rather tepid, cup of tea.

§

As she walked home alone later, having declined Humphrey's offer to accompany her, Ruth reflected bitterly on what she could only see as a failed opportunity. Her natural loquaciousness and ebullience had quite deserted her. She had sat there like a little mouse, saying almost nothing, speaking when spoken to. What could the Naylands think of her? A little country simpleton with nowt in her noggin but straw and giggles. Not the sort of girl they'd want their Humphrey consorting with. The only ray of hope seemed to come from Molly. Ruth sensed a kindred spirit and, as she turned into the lane leading to the farm she resolved to try and speak again to Humphrey's sister under less formal circumstances.

CHAPTER FOUR

MOLLY

Of all the Nayland children, Molly was the least conventional, although on the surface she usually appeared to conform very closely to the stereotype of a young woman of her class. Her formal education had been confined to attendance at the elementary school in the village which all her siblings had also attended. Thereafter the improvement of her mind had proceeded more informally, but she had inherited her father's interest in history and love of literature and had become, like him, an avid reader. Moulded as a child by the works of the Misses Austen and Bronte, she had nonetheless retained a slightly cynical view of the status of women in her society, and had of late also been influenced by the Pankhursts and their sisterhood.

Like many, she had been shocked and thrilled by the sensational event at the previous year's Derby when a suffragette, Emily Davison, ran in front of the King's horse, 'Anmer', as it rounded Tattenham Corner. Emily was dreadfully injured and died later, a martyr to her cause. Molly felt a surge of bitter-sweet elation, although her admiration for Emily's courage was mitigated by her concern for the horse and the jockey, both of whom were also brought to ground. It would be better, she reflected, if one could make one's grand gestures without endangering the innocent. Fortunately 'Anmer', though doubtless bewildered, was unhurt, and his jockey suffered no injury other than a mild concussion.

It was not surprising that Molly and Humphrey were very close. Oliver and Gertrude were almost an older generation, and their other brother, Archie, two years Molly's senior, had died in infancy. The two youngest Naylands ate together, played together and fought together from the earliest times they could remember. They were each other's strongest ally and best friend. Their list of battle honours was long – sneaking out of the Vicarage late at night so they could watch the huge bonfire up on the fell to celebrate the relief of Mafeking, pilfering apples from a neighbour's orchard (Molly on watch, Humphrey climbing the trees).

"We'd never have done it," said Molly to her furious father when their crime came to light, "if he hadn't said that we were never to go into his orchard and he'd tan our hides if he saw us there. Anyway," she went on, "it wasn't Piglet's fault. I made him do it!"

The Vicar rightly disbelieved this, and administered to both children one of his very infrequent beatings which they bore uncomplainingly.

The episode of the mouse was more successful. Discovered by the children in its nest behind the chicken coop, it was transferred temporarily to an old biscuit tin and then surreptitiously released by Molly in the drawing-room to the considerable consternation and dismay of a meeting of the Women's Institute which was taking place there. Responding to the shrieks and cries of distress, Humphrey had come to the rescue and earned the eternal gratitude of the ladies of the parish by recapturing the little interloper. It was later restored to its home near the chickens with a reward of some bread crumbs and fragments of cheese.

Molly had wept bitter tears when it was time for Humphrey to go away to boarding school, and she lived for the holidays when they could resume their alliance.

Humphrey's illness had been in several ways a life-changing experience for Molly. It was the first time anyone close to her had ridden into the Valley of the Shadow of Death since the passing of

Archie of which she had been too small to retain any memory. This kind of experience always brings one to contemplate one's own mortality and the harsh arbitrariness of Nature's laws. But it also gave her for the first time a strong sense of what she might do with her life. Up to that point she had seemed to face a choice between the prosaic prospects of her current situation as a dutiful daughter and a potential helpmeet and consort for some tedious local worthy, and the intriguing but unspecified possibilities hinted at in the tracts of the Women's Suffrage movement. Now those possibilities had a real face.

The crisis that gripped the family through Humphrey's dice with death had brought forth a strong response from everybody, but none more than Molly, partly because of her closeness to him and partly because, as she said herself, "I haven't got anything better to do," and she, more than anyone, could take the credit for his survival. Not only was she a tireless nurse, at his bed-side at all hours with water, towels, bed-pans, basins and the like, but her ferocious determination must have communicated itself to him. Humphrey could recall one little vignette shining through the foggy pall of pain and fever with Molly seated by his bed clasping his hand tightly in hers, her pale face set and blue eyes blazing.

"Piglet you are **not** going to die! Do you hear me? You are **not**! If you do I shall never forgive you as long as I live!"

And, as it turned out, he had not.

For Molly, the realization that, not only was she good at the business of caring for an invalid, but that she actually enjoyed it, was a revelation. She discovered a copy of Florence Nightingale's *Notes on Nursing* tucked away in a bookshelf in her father's study and had devoured the contents avidly, and a friend in York had managed to get her hands on Clara Barton's *Story of the Red Cross*. For the first time Molly felt that her life might have a purpose and a focus and, now that Humphrey's need had abated, she was resolved to pursue the ideal, despite what she shrewdly suspected might be opposition from the rest of her family.

Meanwhile, family life went on, with its little intrigues and challenges. Knowing him as she did, Molly was instinctively aware that Humphrey's new-found relationship with Ruth was more than just a casual encounter. Having grown up in family intimacy with his sisters and mother, Humphrey was quite comfortable in female company, but had hitherto shown no signs of amorous inclinations. The various girls and young women he had met had aroused nothing more than jocular friendliness. He had never been tempted to follow Oliver's example in breaking out of his school dormitory late at night to keep an assignation with a local lovely in the nearby city of York. Ruth was clearly different, and Molly had to admit to a pang of jealousy which she instantly repressed as unworthy of her. Molly herself had been the target of numerous respectful (and a few disrespectful) advances over the years from lads in the village and friends of her brothers who had come to stay. These she had, with one notable exception, firmly repulsed, and that exception could perhaps be excused as a childhood crush.

However, to say she had a soft spot for Oliver's old school chum Marcus would be a considerable understatement. Their last meeting had been a good many years previously on Marcus' last visit to England when he spent a number of weeks at the vicarage. Molly had then been thirteen, a very susceptible age, as her mother had pointed out. The tanned and debonair young man from the colonies might have stepped right out of the pages of the romantic novels that were then her standard literary fare, and she had hung around the two young men until Oliver, in exasperation, had besought his mother to warn her off. Marcus was handsome, charming and funny, but also invariably proper and courteous. "If only I was older!" Molly would lament bitterly to herself. Even at that age, had he proposed (which of course would never have occurred to him), she would have accepted in a heart-beat and damned the consequences. As it was, he returned to Africa and went out of her life, although he fanned the embers over the years by never failing to include a jocular message for her in his fairly regular letters to her brother. She had wept secret tears at the news of his marriage to a South African society beauty, and had, equally secretly, rejoiced when, after a couple of years, the marriage had broken down. Now, at the grand old age of twenty-two, she could recognize her juvenile infatuation for what it was, but still retained a fond image of her 'wild colonial boy', against whom her contemporary suitors were measured and invariably found wanting. At the same time, she could understand the strength of the feelings Humphrey evidently had for Ruth and acknowledge that, as he was not just a child, they might be more than mere infatuation.

Molly helped her mother clear up the tea things after Ruth had left.

"She seems a nice enough girl," said Louisa. "Didn't have much to say for herself, though."

"I expect she found it bit overwhelming, Ma. Can you remember how you felt when you met Pa's parents for the first time?"

"Well, yes, dear, but that wasn't the same thing at all. I was his intended. Do you really think Humphrey is that serious about this girl?"

"I haven't talked to him about it Ma, but – yes. I think he is. And her name," she added gently, "is Ruth!"

"Well, I think it's very peculiar," said her mother firmly. "Humphrey's never shown any interest in girls. He's only a boy. He's just out of school. He doesn't need to be bothering with this sort of thing. It's very unsuitable. I shall get your father to speak to him."

§

It was two days later that Molly had to go down to the village to purchase something from the shop. As she came out she saw Ruth standing across the street. As soon as the other girl caught sight of Molly she came across and greeted her.

"Good morning, Miss Nayland. I wonder if I might have a

word?"

"Of course," said Molly. She glanced quizzically at Ruth, who looked somehow at the same time embarrassed and determined. This meeting, she decided, was no accident.

"Shall we sit on the Parkes bench? And Ruth, please call me Molly. 'Miss Nayland' makes me feel like an old woman!"

Ruth smiled nervously."Aye, I will, if that's alright."

The two girls crossed the road to the village green and sat on the solid wooden bench beside it. Stoutly made of heavy oak, it was inscribed with the words 'In loving memory of Alfred Parkes, Churchwarden of this parish from 1871 to 1903. Servant of many, friend to all.'

"What was it you wanted to tell me, Ruth?"

The younger girl paused for a few seconds before answering. She seemed to be gathering her courage or perhaps choosing her words carefully.

"T'other day, when I came round for a cuppa, I don't know what came over me. There was so much I wanted to say, and I just sat there like a sack of straw. I don't know what you can have thought."

"Don't worry, Ruth. I can quite understand. You must have found us very intimidating."

"Oh, it weren't that. Your Mam were ever so nice, and so were you. I just got all tied up. I had all these thoughts in my head, that I needed to bring out and I couldn't. I'm not usually short of a word." She smiled wryly and dropped her eyes. "Humphrey could tell you."

"You're very fond of Humphrey, aren't you?"

Ruth raised her head and looked steadily into Molly's sympathetic blue eyes.

"Aye, I am," she said softly. "I never met anyone like him. He's so sweet. I never have trouble talking with him." She laughed. "I s'pose that's why I wanted to see you. To explain that I'm not just a sackless barmpot. I hoped you might put in a word for me with your folks."

Molly felt a pang of concern. She remembered all too clearly her mother's most recent pronouncement on the subject of this relationship. She reached forward and put her gloved hand on Ruth's.

"I'll do everything I can, Ruth, I promise. But, you know, Humphrey's very young. They want him to go up to Oxford and have all the opportunities that he can to, well, get an education, prepare for life."

"Oh, so do I," said Ruth earnestly. " He says he wants to stay here but I tell him he mustn't. It's a wonderful chance. I don't want to hold him back. Then there's all this talk of war."

"Oh, that's tosh!" said Molly firmly, with a confidence she didn't really feel. "It's just a lot of sabre-rattling by the great powers. We'd never go to war with Germany. Why, the King and the Kaiser are cousins!"

"Well, that's as maybe, but I've known cousins as couldn't bide each other."

"Anyway, you're not to worry." On an impulse she leaned forward again and said, "I'm glad Humphrey's met you. I'll do my best to make Ma and Pa feel the same!"

§

As it happened, the first person Molly ran into on her return home was Humphrey.

"Hallo, Piglet. I've just been talking with your Ruth."

"Really?" Humphrey looked a bit startled. "What did you talk about?"

"This and that. You! I think she was worried that she hadn't made a good impression when she came round the other day."

"Yes, well, she might be right," said Humphrey gloomily. "Pa says he wants to have a chat with me in his study after dinner and it must be about that. I know for a fact he's finished this week's sermon, so it won't be asking me to help him with that." He gave a short laugh. The Vicar regarded his sermons as entirely his responsibility, and only very occasionally consulted his wife on their wording. The rest of the family only heard the finished product.

"I'm not going to stop seeing Ruth just because they don't approve. What do you think of her, Moll?"

"I think she's lovely!" Molly placed her hand on his arm and smiled up at him. "You have my full support!"

"Thanks, Moll. I think I'm going to need it!"

CHAPTER FIVE

AUBREY

The Reverend Aubrey Nayland regarded himself as a lucky man. He was familiar with the dicta of the Roman historian, Livy, who had once said,'Men are slower to recognize blessings than misfortunes' but did not consider this applied to him. Vicar of the church of St Cuthbert's at Cowdenhall for more than 25 years, he had a job he loved, working among people most of whom he liked and respected. His occupation gave him plenty of time for the pastimes he chiefly enjoyed – reading, philosophical discussion, and rambling through the English countryside. He lived in what he believed to be the most beautiful part of the finest country on earth. He saw himself as truly blessed.

He also saw himself as most fortunate in his immediate family – a wife who was a loving and loyal support, children who had, by and large, grown into decent and likeable human beings with whom he had a mutually respectful and loving relationship. There had, indeed, been some bumps on the smooth road of child-rearing: the death of little Archie and the sorrow this had caused his wife had deeply grieved him too, and some of Oliver's more outrageous escapades had engendered in both of his parents a good deal of disquiet and anxiety. However, the passing years had dulled the pain of loss, and there was every evidence, with Oliver's engagement to Mary Elizabeth, that his feckless youth was behind him. This latest difficulty with Humphrey was a problem that, he had no doubt, could be solved. He shared Livy's view that 'many difficulties that nature throws in our way may be smoothed away by the exercise of intelligence.'

When father and son met in the Vicar's study after dinner, they sat for a minute or two in a somewhat uneasy contemplation of the night falling across the fields visible through the windows beyond the Vicarage garden. Aubrey eventually broke the silence.

"Your mother and I are a bit worried about your liaison with Albert Moffat's daughter."

"What do you mean, Father, liaison?"

"Well, you seem to be spending a great deal of time in her company."

"If I am, where's the harm in that?"

The Vicar didn't answer immediately. He needed to muster his thoughts. He realized this might be a delicate moment.

"Humphrey, there's nothing wrong with associating with young women – perfectly natural, normal. After all," he laughed nervously, "one day I expect you'll marry one. It's just that at your age it isn't healthy to spend all your time with just one young woman."

"But she's the only one I want to spend my time with! What's wrong with her? Is it because she doesn't talk the same way we do?"

"Well, not exactly, but she does come from a very different background. You would have very little in common."

"That's just where you're wrong, father. We have everything in common, all the important things anyway. You don't need to be exactly the same. You and mother approved of Mackenzie marrying Gertie and he's a foreigner!"

"No, Humphrey, not really. He's a Canadian, and Canada is part of the British Empire. He is also a mature gentleman, a man of substance, who can provide for Gertrude in every way, although I must say," he added in a conscious attempt to introduce a note of levity that might be expected to draw his son's sympathy, "I should greatly prefer it if he were less devoted to the Empire of the Lord."

"That's the point, isn't it?" said Humphrey earnestly, ignoring the proffered olive branch. "She's not from our class, she doesn't talk like we do, her dad is a working man. Father! This is the twentieth century! That sort of thing doesn't matter any more! Or it jolly well shouldn't!"

Aubrey realized that the conversation was going nowhere pleasant and that the time had come for a tactical retreat. He leant forward and put his hand on Humphrey's knee.

"My dear chap, I understand your loyalty. I think it is admirable that we stand up for our friends. Could I just beg that you think about what I have said? One of the few advantages of getting on in years is that one can often see things more clearly, from a wider perspective. I know you may find this difficult to accept. As Terence tells us 'What harsh judges fathers are to all young men.'

Humphrey was not much mollified. "I know you and Ma mean well, but you just don't understand."

§

As they prepared for bed that night, the Vicar reported to Louisa the unsatisfactory conversation with their son. They agreed that Aubrey should speak to Albert who must surely be just as aware of the situation as they were and, they supposed, equally disapproving. The opportunity arose after church the next day.

The farmer approached Reverend Nayland after the service to return with thanks two of the books he had been lent.

"Thank you, Albert," said Aubrey. "I do hope you found them interesting. I wonder if I might have a word?"

"Aye, Vicar." Albert turned to Ruth. "You go on home with Emily, luv. I'll be there directly."

The two men re-entered the church and went through to the vestry. Aubrey placed the books on the table and cleared his throat nervously.

"Albert, it's about Humphrey…"

"And our Ruth? Aye, I've been thinking on that meself. They're that thick, and I don't think it's right. I've spoken to Ruth about it, but it's made no difference. Bairns today, they don't pay no mind to what they're told by their parents. Not like when we were, lads, Vicar. It might have been different if my old lass were with us, but she isn't, and that's that."

Aubrey felt an immense relief. He had not relished the thought of a confrontation with his old friend, and this now seemed unlikely.

"Louisa and I have been most concerned lately. Not that we have anything against Ruth," he added hastily. "She seems a delightful young girl. But it's just not right for them to have this … " he groped for the word, "... obsession with each other. They're so young. There is so much they need to do with their lives. I don't think they understand what the world is really about."

"You've hit nail on the head, Vicar. They just don't know. And it's up to us to make sure they find out." He paused and scratched the side of his face.

"Is your lad still planning on going to the university?"

"Oh! Undoubtedly! But that won't be until September. And, of course, he'll be coming home during his vacations, I expect. Still, perhaps a few months apart will bring the young people to their senses."

"Aye, mebbe." Albert didn't sound convinced. "Any road, I'll have another word with our Ruth now I've had a chat with 'ee. Perhaps she'll see it differently."

The two men stood in contemplative silence for a few seconds, and then Aubrey grasped his friend's hand.

"I'm so glad we had this talk, Albert, and that you and I see eye to eye on this. I'll think about what is best to do. Louisa will have some good ideas, I'm sure." He laughed wryly. "Women are so much better at this sort of thing."

Aubrey recovered the books and the men walked in companionable silence out of the vestry and down the aisle to the entrance of the church. A very light drizzle had started to fall so, after a final firm hand-shake, both hastened to their respective dwellings.

§

After the usual Sunday roast (lamb, with potatoes, carrots and parsnips) Aubrey and Louisa retreated to the Vicar's study where he told her about his meeting with Albert Moffat.

"I think he is as worried as we are," said Aubrey. "He knows this is not the right thing for either of these young people, at least not at this point in their lives. He'll talk to his Ruth and I'll have to have another chat with Humphrey."

"Do you think that'll do any good, dear?"

"Probably not," replied the Vicar gloomily. "In this day and age I can hardly forbid him to see her. He's not a baby any more. I suppose we should be grateful that he has hitherto been much more circumspect in his personal life than Oliver."

Louisa bridled at this. If she had a flaw in her otherwise admirably pragmatic and sensible outlook, it was her adamant reluctance to believe ill of her elder son.

"I don't think that's fair, dear. Their characters are so different. Oliver had a great deal of high spirits that he needed to work off. In any case, he has settled down beautifully now, or he very soon will."

The Vicar decided against worrying at this particular bone of contention. In the course of a long, and generally very happy, married life, he had learned which arguments he was likely to win and which were, in any case, worth engaging in.

"I think what we need is to find some way of diverting him. He will be going up to BNC in the autumn, but that won't be for another four months." Brasenose College, Oxford – BNC to its familiars – was the Vicar's own *alma mater*, and his status as a well-respected alumnus had been instrumental in securing Humphrey's admission to its membership and, when he became so ill, getting the college's agreement to defer this admission for twelve months. "Moreover," he went on, "he'll be coming home for vacations so it isn't as though they'll be completely out of touch. Still, Oxford is a different world, almost a foreign country. I expect it'll change his ideas about life. It certainly did mine. He may come to see his attachment to this girl for what it is, just an immature infatuation."

"You may be right," replied his wife. "I hope you are. I'm not so sure. Molly thinks he is very serious about her."

"Molly?" said the Vicar indignantly. "Molly? She's little more than a child herself. What does she know?"

"Well, she knows Humphrey better than anyone," responded his wife calmly. "I would not be dismissing her opinion out of hand." They sat in silence for a while.

"D'you know," said Louisa suddenly, "your mentioning a foreign country just gave me an idea. Do you remember the Guscotts at Whitby?"

"I don't think so," said Aubrey doubtfully. "Should I?"

"Of course you do!" said Louisa firmly. "Their eldest son, George, got involved with a most unsuitable woman down in London."

"Ah, yes! I remember it now. Ten years older than him and a divorcee. Terrible scandal! Whatever happened to him?"

"They sent him off to America. Sir Charles has a brother in Baltimore or Washington or somewhere so George went and stayed with him for a few months and by the time he got back his lady friend had her talons into someone else and the whole thing died a natural death. Enid Simpson was telling me all about it at the WI meeting."

"But we don't know anyone in America," objected Aubrey.

"No, but there is Marcus."

"In South Africa?"

"Yes. And that's even further away than America!"

"He'd have to defer Oxford again."

"Yes, but I'm sure that the college would agree to that if you went and spoke nicely to the Dean."

Aubrey had not been married to Louisa for more than 35 years without developing the ability to read her mind. He glanced across at her and smiled.

"You're still worried about him signing up if there is a war, aren't you?" The war fever, stirred up by bellicose statements from the French earlier in the year, had abated considerably in recent weeks, and the general view (outside the likes of Oliver and his cronies) was that the imminent danger was past.

"Well, naturally I shouldn't want him to get involved in something as futile as that," said Louisa firmly, "but I'm sure there isn't going to be a war. And anyhow," she added rather illogically, "it'll all be over by Christmas, Oliver says."

"And how will we persuade Humphrey to go?" enquired his father. "No doubt young Guscott's parents could threaten to cut off his inheritance or something if he didn't go. I'm not sure that we have that sort of weapon in our armoury."

"Perhaps if the invitation were to come from Marcus? He's always writing to Oliver about these wonderful business opportunities out there. He could say that there is some especially attractive scheme for which he needs the help of someone he can trust."

The Vicar rubbed his nose. "I don't like the idea of asking someone to say something that isn't strictly true."

"But, dear, it doesn't need to be untrue. Marcus is always coming up with splendid projects. As you know, he tried to persuade Oliver to join him in a couple of them a few years ago."

"I suppose that is true," Aubrey admitted.

"So will you write to him about it?"

The Vicar pondered the question. "I'll think about it," he said at length.

CORRESPONDENCE – 1

Rev A Nayland
The Vicarage
Cowdenhall
Yorkshire

April 1914

Dear Reverend Nayland

I do apologise for not having responded to your letter before now. I was out on a training camp with the company and did not receive it until I returned to Bulawayo yesterday.

I must say that I was greatly intrigued by its contents and to learn that it is necessary for young Humphrey to temporarily absent himself from the land of his birth. It is hard to imagine what could have given rise to this situation for one who I have always been informed, and indeed recall from my own knowledge, albeit some years ago, to be of exemplary character. Perhaps it has something to do with his recent illness from which I understood him to have entirely recovered.

In any case, that is no concern of mine and I shall be happy, given my long friendship with Oliver and the great kindness and hospitality I have always enjoyed from your family, to do whatever is in my power to help.

As it happens, several interesting business propositions have arisen in the past few months to which, as a result of my enrolment in the BSAP, I have been unable to make any personal commitment. I shall, at the earliest opportunity, make enquiries to discover whether these may hold some likely attraction for Humphrey and, if so, shall, as you suggest, write to him about them.

It would, in any event, be a very great pleasure to welcome a Nayland out here. I abandoned some years ago my attempts to lure Oliver out to share my portion of the 'white man's burden', and I fear that your younger daughter clearly remains indifferent to the large number of cattle and goats which I would been happy to make over to yourself and with which I feel sure you would have been well satisfied!

Joking apart, it really will be a delight if Humphrey is able to make the journey. I should warn you, though, that there must always be a strong likelihood that he will, as I did, succumb to the fatal charm of Africa and be unwilling to return to you.

Please convey my best considerations to Mrs Nayland and, of course to Oliver, to whom I shall be writing very shortly.

Your very affectionate

Marcus Graythorpe

c/o BSAP Depot
Jameson Street
Bulawayo

CHAPTER SIX

HUMPHREY

There was one walk that Ruth and Humphrey used to take often that was, perhaps, their favourite. It began off the lane near the Moffat farm and skirted one of their meadows before crossing a little brook and meandering through quite dense woodland. It was here that they had seen the wild man, what now seemed an age ago. Halfway through the wood there was a small clearing with a conveniently-placed fallen tree on which they could talk, or kiss, or simply sit, holding hands, in the unspoken warmth of their intimacy. They sat there now, looking at the bluebells which stretched in glorious profusion away under the shadows of the trees. A rabbit hopped into view at the end of the clearing and sat there for a few moments, ears pricked and nose whiffling busily, before it detected their presence and bounded away into the undergrowth.

Humphrey held Ruth's hand in both of his, examining it as though he were searching for some blemish or imperfection that he knew must be there but could not be located.

"I shall have to go, Ruthie" he said sadly.

"But why Humphrey?" she pleaded, squeezing his hand and peering up into his troubled face.

He didn't answer straight away. Then he turned and looked directly into her eyes.

"Because I must. It's a wonderful opportunity, it'll be a terrific experience, I'll be helping out a family friend. Mother and Father are both tremendously keen on the idea. It'll only be for a short time. Once the business is on its feet, I'll come straight home. To you." He leaned forward and kissed her softly.

"And what does Molly think?"

Humphrey smiled wryly. "She's not so keen. She thinks they're just trying to get me out of the way."

"And do you think that?"

Humphrey pondered the matter.

"No, I don't think so. I think it really is a good opportunity and I'd be daft to turn it down. I'm sure they would like us to be apart for a while, and I know mother still worries about a war coming and me getting involved. But I don't think that's the main reason. Anyway, it's not forever. I can still go to Oxford at the end of next year, Father says. And you'll still be here, won't you?" He looked earnestly into her face.

"Of course I will! Always!" They kissed again. "When must you go?"

"They've booked me on a boat from Liverpool in three weeks' time."

"Oh! Humphrey! That's no time at all!" She sounded desperate and Humphrey felt a bitter pang of regret. How could he do this to the person who had come to matter more to him than anyone else? He did not know the answer to that question. They sat for a while not speaking and then Ruth suddenly looked at his watch and gasped.

"Oh my! Look at the time! I must be home!" They got up from their seat on the log and walked swiftly back the way they had come. Just before they emerged from the wood, Humphrey stopped and turned to Ruth, putting his hands on her shoulders as he gazed earnestly into her eyes. He felt an almost overwhelming surge of love and pain.

"Ruthie, I promise, whatever happens, that I'll come back and I won't ever forget you. Do you believe me?"

She held his gaze for a long moment and then, wordlessly hugged him as tight as she was able.

§

The next days went by with quite amazing speed for Humphrey. His life had never before been driven to quite the same extent by an immutable deadline. His existence had always proceeded at a leisurely pace, changes, like the seasons, happening gradually with plenty of time for adjustment. Now he was having to deal with the fact of an imminent upheaval that was going to wrench him away from everything that was familiar to him – the scenery, the climate, the animals, the way of life. What little he knew about Africa came from what he had read – Rider Haggard's *'King Solomon's Mines'*, Henry Morton Stanley's *'How I found Livingstone'*, and, above all, Percy Fitzpatrick's classic, *'Jock of the Bushveld'*, that marvelous reminiscence of life in Transvaal in the latter stages of the 19th Century, before the country was torn apart by the Boer War. He had been captivated by the tale of the heroic bull-terrier and his master as they coped with the challenges of life on what was then a frontier of civilization, their encounters with the wild animals and the hardly less wild humans that were to be found there. He had been thrilled by the stories of big-game hunting and inspired by the many characters whose paths Jock and his master had crossed. These included Rocky, the taciturn American mountain man, full of priceless wisdom gruffly imparted, his eyes always dreamily focused on some far horizon, who one day had simply shouldered his pack and set off for that horizon without any explanation and with just a wave of the hand and a brief "so long."

Another of Jock's friends to have captured Humphrey's imagination was Jim, the Zulu, a mighty warrior now reduced to menial work for the white man, but whose pride and manly self-respect lay just beneath the surface. Jim had fought at Isandlhwana, where the redcoats were cut off and massacred by the Zulu impis, and a few days later at Rorke's Drift where the indomitable courage of a handful of British soldiers, and the murderous efficiency of modern weaponry, had stemmed the tide. Jim had also been at Ulundi where the might of the Zulu nation was smashed for ever. Humphrey had never even seen a black man, let alone spoken to one, but he felt that, through the pages of Jock's story, he would recognize the people when he met them if, indeed, they were still the same as those Fitzpatrick had described.

The greatest effect of the change, though, would be, he knew, not so much the embracing of the new but the abandonment of the old. True, he had been subjected to some upheaval when, at the age of 13, he had gone away to boarding school. However, his life there, though very different to home, was not entirely unfamiliar. He could still remember Oliver's own tales of life at St Peter's, and those of other boys of his acquaintance who had gone away to that or similar schools. Moreover, York was only a short train ride away and, though much was different to home, much was the same – the language, the moral code, the church services, the newspapers. He was able to return home for the holidays, which occupied a significant part of the year, and was usually able to sleep in his bed at the Vicarage at least once during each term, over the half-term break. Postal communication was almost immediate and, though, like most schoolboys, Humphrey had hardly been a diligent and regular correspondent, it had been comforting to receive frequent and up-to-date news from home and to know that appeals to the family for help, advice, or provisions to render school life bearable, would reach their destination within a day or two at most.

Africa was going to be different. To judge from the correspondence received over the years from Marcus, letters could take three weeks or more to arrive, and there was clearly no possibility of coming home for the weekend.

Apart from his time at school, Humphrey had spent his entire life in the company of his parents and Molly, and now he was to be separated from them for months, maybe longer. His school experiences told him this would be hard. The parting from Ruth, however, was going to be on quite another plane. She was the first person outside his family with whom he had built up a really strong personal relationship. Although he had many friends at school, with none of them had he been a soul mate, a confidant. Perhaps because of his special bond with Molly, perhaps because of a natural reticence as the youngest in a large family full of strong, outgoing personalities, he had not felt any need to for that sort of friendship and so it had never happened.

With Ruth, though, he had from the first felt a strong affinity. She was someone he enjoyed talking to, someone whose opinions he sought and respected, someone to whom he had no hesitation in unburdening himself. The only person remotely like her in that respect was Molly. And underlying it all was the sexual element. Humphrey was, in many ways, something of an innocent, probably not untypical of boys of his age and class. He was not unaware of the 'facts of life' and had, as much through witnessing his brother's exploits as anything else, seen how these primal urges played out in human behaviour. Hitherto, though, he had been a detached and relatively dispassionate observer. Now he was involved as passionately as it was possible to be. Everything about Ruth was either thrilling or delightful or both. He loved the tender curve of her cheek and throat, the tanned neatness of her ankles. He adored her little mannerisms – the way she would bite her lower lip when she was puzzled or concentrating, how she raised her hand to her chin whenever she saw something beautiful or amazing, how she would sometimes give a little skip in her walk, like a small child, when she was especially happy. He cherished the little lock of hair which would invariably escape from its fellows when she tied her hair back and would hang over her brow to be absently (and uselessly) pushed back into place. The grave stillness of her beautiful face when she was listening to something solemn, the happy radiance when she smiled, the warmth when she would impulsively reach forward and squeeze his arm, filled him with aching joy. He had no benchmark against which to measure the quality of Ruth's embraces, if the Valentine's Day episode could be dismissed as irrelevant, but he could not believe that they were anything less than perfect. The eager softness of her kiss, the urgent but tender clasp of her arms about him, the way she strained her lovely body against his, all awoke in him the strongest emotions he had ever experienced. It is said that mutual desire is the strongest aphrodisiac, and Humphrey had little doubt that Ruth's feelings for him matched his for her. How was he ever going to be able to leave her behind to go forward to an uncertain future, however exciting and new it might seem? The prospect filled him with a sick dread.

§

The day before Humphrey's departure dawned fine and warm, yet another perfect day in what had been an almost perfect summer. Ruth had been adamant that she would not come and see him off at the station. He had to get an early train to York to catch the boat train to Liverpool where the Kenilworth Castle would be already docked, preparing to sail for Cape Town the next day. They had arranged for him to slip over to the farm and meet her in the evening, but in the end it was past dark by the time the Naylands had enjoyed what Molly gloomily described as 'the last supper' and Humphrey was able to get away.

"I just want a last walk around the village before I go," he had said and there had been no demur, although Molly gave him a rather strange and, he thought, knowing look.

The farm was dark when he got there except for a flicker of light at the kitchen window and, when he peered in he could see Ruth sitting reading by the light of a lantern. Of her father and Emily there was no sign. Presumably they had already retired.

He tapped lightly on the window-pane and Ruth immediately came to the door which she closed behind her. Hand in hand they felt their way cautiously down the lane. Shortly, the full moon emerged from behind a cloud and bathed the scene in a ghostly light. Humphrey glanced down at the girl beside him. She was wearing a plain white blouse with a long dark skirt that he seemed to recognize from church. She had a shawl around her shoulders: although it had been a warm day, the temperature had dropped once the sun went down and there was a little bit of a chill in the wind.

"Where shall we go?" he whispered.

"Up on't fell," she replied in a normal voice, and gave his arm a squeeze. "No need to whisper, juggins. There's nobody'll hear us." In this she was not entirely correct. As they went through a gate into the field that led to the top of the farm, a badger emerged from under the hedge and paused for a moment, looking at them, Humphrey thought, rather crossly, before jogging off about his business. In a few minutes they reached their goal, a flat boulder at the top of the field above the farm where they had often sat before. From this vantage point they had a panoramic view of the valley and, in the bright moonlight, were able to pick out many little landmarks along their journey together - the field where Gertie had broken her collar-bone, the wild man's wood, and Ballard's Bridge where they had leaned on the parapet, dropping sticks into the water and watching the minnows dart about in the shallows.

After a while they stopped talking and just sat there, close together, lost in their thoughts. A gust of breeze came up the valley and the scene was plunged back into darkness as the moon slipped behind a cloud.

"Are you cold?" asked Humphrey.

"No. Yes. Maybe!" Ruth gave a little laugh and snuggled up closer to him. They sat there for a while longer before Humphrey stirred.

"I think I'd better go. They'll be wondering what's become of me."

"What did you tell them?"

"I said I wanted a last walk around the village by myself."

"Do you think they believed you?"

"I don't know. I don't think Molly did. She gave me one of her looks."

He turned and looked down at her face, visible once more with the re-emergence of the moon.

"You can always talk to Moll, Ruthie. She understands." The girl nodded without speaking. Then she got to her feet and pulled on his arm.

"Come on then. Best be gone."

Humphrey stood up and then, holding her hand in one of his, pointed with the other at the night sky.

"See the moon, Ruthie. Wherever we are, we'll be under that same moon. I'll look up at it and know that you'll be looking at it too. Even when we're miles apart, we can feel close to each other."

They walked back down the field in silence. Humphrey glanced down at the girl beside him. Her eyes were downcast and her face inscrutable.

When they reached the shadow of the barn near the farm gate they stopped.

"We'd best say our goodbyes properly here," he said softly.

Without another word they embraced. Ruth's shawl slipped unnoticed to the ground. For a while it seemed that time stood still. Nothing existed beyond their all-consuming passion, longing, agony. After what seemed an age but was probably less than a minute, Ruth suddenly disengaged.

"What is it, Ruthie?" Humphrey asked, looking down at her in concern. She said nothing but looked at him steadfastly for a few seconds. Then she seemed to make up her mind.

"Come," she said, taking his hand and going to the barn door. Once inside, the cattle peered round inquisitively and the chickens clucked in vague alarm from their perches. Ruth closed the door behind them and led Humphrey to the back of the barn where a number of sheaves of straw were stacked. Some had fallen over and made a rough platform just above the floor.

Ruth turned to face him. Her face was lit by the moonlight beaming in from the window at the top of the barn, but the rest of her was in shadow. She looked very grave, serious. Then she did something entirely unexpected and amazing. She took his left hand in both of hers and placed it on her breast. Humphrey was electrified. Through the thin material of the blouse his fingers could feel the warmth of her body and the hardness of her nipple pressed against his palm.

"Humphrey," she said gently but clearly, "I want you to luv me."

For a moment he was paralysed and his throat was so constricted he couldn't speak. His left hand remained where it was. At last he was able to croak a response.

"What do mean?" he gasped.

"You know what I mean," Ruth said softly. He did.

"Are you sure, Ruthie?"

"Yes, I'm sure."

§

For the rest of his life Humphrey could recall in the minutest detail everything that happened that evening in the Moffat barn. Ruth turned and fetched an old horse-blanket hanging over a rail at the side of the barn and laid it over the straw. She kicked off her shoes and came and stood in front of him and, without taking her eyes from his, she undid the buttons on her blouse and laid it aside. Then she unhitched her skirt, let it fall to the ground and stepped out of it. Her camisole and knickers joined it on the floor of the barn. Humphrey had stood frozen but he then made to start undoing his own clothes. Ruth stopped him.

"No!" she said quietly but firmly. Still looking him in the eyes, she undid his shirt, unbuckled his belt and the buttons on his trousers. He also kicked off his shoes and stepped away from his trousers. He placed his hands on her bare shoulders and noticed she was trembling.

"Are you sure, Ruthie?" he asked again.

"Oh yes! Please!"

His shirt, vest and underpants joined his other clothing on the floor and, with a strength he hadn't known he possessed, he lifted her up and laid her down on the blanket. For a brief second they gazed at each other in the moonlight and then their bodies could hold back no more.

Afterwards they lay together entwined, her head on his chest and his free hand gently caressing the sweet curve of her waist. He softly kissed the top of her head.

"Is it always as wonderful as that?" he whispered. She turned her head up and kissed him.

"Oh Humphrey! I hope so. I do hope so!"

CORRESPONDENCE – 2

Mrs Louisa Nayland
The Vicarage
Cowdenhall
Yorkshire   *August 1914*
Dearest mother

I very much hope you received the letters I posted when the ship called at Las Palmas. I wrote to Oliver and Molly as well as to you and father, but I did send them all to the Vicarage because I wasn't quite certain of Oliver's address at Catterick.

You will be glad to know that, after those first few dreadful days, I have quite got my sea-legs and now do not feel sick at all. This is just as well as there is always lots to do and you can't enjoy it if you're feeling wretched. There are organised games of deck quoits and table tennis and one afternoon we even played cricket on the deck, though with a tennis ball, not a real cricket ball. Some fellows have been doing gymnastic exercises every morning, though I have so far managed to avoid that!

The evenings are always busy too with housey-housey, cards and concerts. I was persuaded, much against my better judgement, to join a chorus at one of the concerts. We sang the Policemen's Chorus from the Pirates of Penzance which I'm sure you will remember from that production we saw in York the Christmas before last. I managed to stay in the background so that my complete lack of musical ability went unnoticed, and it seemed to go well. At any rate, the audience applauded at the end (though perhaps in relief because we had finished).

On several evenings the ship's company have organised a dance for the passengers which has been very jolly. The ship has its own band and very good they are too. The officers are always there in force, looking very smart in their white uniforms and are much in demand by the young ladies among the passengers. I have no doubt that, if Molly were here, she could have her pick of handsome sailors. Don't tell her that! I know she'd be furious!

On Sundays they have a service in the main saloon which is usually well attended. The ship's chaplain preaches and his sermons are good deal less inspiring than Father's although, on the positive side, much shorter!

I suppose the main topic of conversation of late has been the troubles in Servia and the possibility of war in the Balkans. Many fellows seem to think that we shall be involved, though I'm not sure I understand why. It's all a very long way from England, and, though the murders of the Archduke and his wife were terrible, I don't see that it's our business. Anyway, no doubt we shall have more news when we get to Cape Town the day after tomorrow.

I'm very much looking forward to seeing Marcus again. I wonder if he has changed much. Perhaps we shan't recognise each other! I'll put this in the post as soon as we arrive and will write again once I know where we are going to be and what is happening.

Give my very best to Father and a pat to Dizzy who I am sure will have already forgotten me!

With much love
Humphrey
On SS Kenilworth Castle   South Atlantic Ocean

CHAPTER SEVEN

MARCUS

As the sun had come up behind Table Mountain that morning it had brought colour, life and warmth to the placid waters of the bay. An observer looking out west into the South Atlantic would have seen the Kenilworth Castle steaming across the silvery ocean to its destination in the Cape Colony. By the time Marcus Graythorpe had made his way down to the docks to meet Humphrey's boat, the mountain had retreated into its usual protective blanket of cloud. Marcus always enjoyed his visits to Cape Town. The towering presence of the mountain, the changing beauty of the bay, sometimes, like now, calm and serene, sometimes whipped into grey fury by the southern winds, the colourful and cosmopolitan crowds that thronged the old streets. He'd had some anxiety that he might not recognize Humphrey who, after all, had been a mere boy when he was last in England. However, he need not have worried. The face of the young man coming down the gangway was unmistakably that of a Nayland. The two men shook hands warmly.

"Good to see you Piglet! And you're looking fit and healthy. How was the voyage?"

"Splendid! At least, after the first few days when I was awfully sick. I'm glad to be here, though. They try and keep you amused on the ship but it does become a bit samey after a while and it'll be nice to get out and about."

"Excellent! Well we can certainly offer you 'out and about' here! How many bags do you have?"

"Just this grip and one cabin trunk. It's got my name painted on."

"Excellent! We'll soon be on our way then." Marcus summoned a porter who was loitering in the background, had a quick word with him, and pressed a coin in his hand.

"He'll get it for us and we can come back here later. They're very efficient unloading the baggage. It won't take long. Are you hungry?"

Humphrey admitted that he wasn't particularly, having had breakfast not long before, so the two men walked a short distance to an inn in a street behind the dock where they ordered drinks and sat down at a table in a corner.

"Well then, young Piglet – or perhaps I should call you Humphrey? – any romantic attachments on board?" Marcus regarded the younger man quizzically over the rim of his tankard.

"No, nothing like that," replied Humphrey, colouring slightly. Marcus laughed.

"Ah well, it does happen, you know! Indeed I met the former Mrs Graythorpe on the boat coming back here in '05. Though I suppose, in the circumstances, that is hardly a recommendation for ship-board romance."

Humphrey changed the subject.

"When are we going to be leaving for Rhodesia?"

"Ah!" said Marcus. "Bit of a change of plan. I expect you've heard the news?"

"What news?"

"Well, we are likely to be at war within the next few days."

"War? With whom?"

"Germany, of course. After that terrible assassination in Servia, the Austrians declared war on Servia, the Russians have declared war on Austria, and Germany has felt obliged to support Austria."

"How does that affect us?"

"Well, France has a treaty with Russia that says they will support the Russians if they are attacked, and you know how much the French hate the Germans. They have been longing for an excuse to go to war with them, and now they've got one. I don't think we have a specific treaty with France, but there seems to be some kind of understanding between us and the French and most well-informed people seem to think that if they go to war, so will we."

"Good gracious!" said Humphrey. "I had no idea it was this serious. I know people were talking about war when I left England, and Oliver has been saying for months that it was coming, but it just seemed a bit unreal. Does this mean you'll be going back to fight?"

"No, no, not at all! They can manage perfectly well without the likes of me and in any case I imagine it would all be over by the time we were able to get there. No, it's German South-West Africa." Humphrey looked mystified.

"German colony north of the Cape. They don't have huge forces there, but I think the Government is worried that they could provide a base for naval operations against our shipping in and out of Cape Town." He took a long pull of his drink. "The other thing they're worried about is that there are plenty of disaffected Dutchmen left over from the South African war and a lot of them fled to South-West Africa. If there is a war with Germany, I think they fear that the German colonial authorities will arm and encourage these people to stir up trouble for us, even maybe restart the war."

"Is that really possible?" asked Humphrey.

"Yes, I think it is. Anyhow the authorities are planning for it, so for the last three weeks we have been on alert and, if war is declared, I would expect that there is a strong possibility that the Union will send a force to South-West Africa, and that might well include the BSAP. So, young Humphrey, I'm stuck down here at the moment and I'm not at all sure when I'll be able to get up to Rhodesia and help you settle in there."

"Perhaps I should stay here until things are a bit clearer," suggested Humphrey.

"Excellent idea!" said Marcus enthusiastically. 'Excellence' was clearly a quality he found in many things. "I have some very good friends who will be happy to put you up for a few days while we decide what to do with you. Let's go back to the wharf and see if they've unloaded your things."

So it was that just a few hours later, Marcus and Humphrey were sitting on the stoep of the Horsfield home in Clifton enjoying an excellent (what else?) English tea served by a smiling black servant in a white uniform and a red tarboosh.

§

Theo Horsfield's career had, in some respects, paralleled Marcus's. He too had come out to the Cape Colony as a soldier and it was during the war that he had struck up a friendship with Marcus who was some years his junior. Like Marcus, he had decided to stay on in South Africa after the war and pursue business opportunities. There the similarity ended, for Theo was a much shrewder businessman and financier than his young friend and his ventures had generally prospered. He was now the principal of a good-sized import/export firm, and doing very well to judge from the size and position of his house and the number and quality of his servants, each one immaculately liveried, pleasant, obsequious and efficient. Marcus was not in the least envious or resentful of his friend's success. His own failures he attributed to circumstances beyond his control and he was blithely confident that, in the fullness of time, the dice would fall his way. Meanwhile he rejoiced that Theo was doing so well.

There was one other respect in which the older man had out-done his friend and that was in the matter of marriage. Like Marcus, Theo had wed a local beauty. Unlike Marcus, though, his union had survived and prospered. He and Nicola had one child, Cornelia, now ten years old and at boarding school in Natal.

Nicola Horsfield, a tall, slim, and elegant woman with short dark hair, was in the process of relating to them the quite entertaining saga of her battle with the gardener on the question of the proper care of rhododendrons, of which some splendid examples fringed their lawn. Marcus had listened to the tale with amusement, but no great fascination. He was not much interested in gardening, unlike Humphrey, who had been able to make some worthwhile contributions, based on his own experiences at home and the knowledge passed on by his mother, whom Marcus knew to be something of a gardening fanatic. As he sipped his tea, Marcus watched Humphrey in conversation and concluded that he possessed that rare ability of being able and willing to really listen to others. Too many people, and Marcus was honest enough to put himself in this category, spent the time when others were speaking in planning what they were going to say next, rather than digesting and evaluating what was being said to them. Humphrey, on the other hand, showed himself to be a most sympathetic listener, always happy to give others a full hearing and to explore their views, only proffering his own when asked or when it was clear that the speaker had said all he or she wanted to.

The saga of the rhododendrons, clearly an unfinished symphony, was interrupted by the return from work of the master of the house. After introductions and the fetching of fresh tea, Theo settled back in his chair.

"I suppose you've heard the latest news?" he asked Marcus.

"And what is that?"

"The French have mobilized!"

"What does that mean?" asked Nicola.

"It means, my dear, that the Frogs have decided that war with Germany is inevitable."

"Does that mean we shall be at war too?"

"I don't see how it can be avoided," her husband replied gloomily. "If the Germans invade France which they surely will if they want a swift victory, they are almost bound to swing round through Belgium, whose neutrality we have guaranteed, so that brings us in. Another thing is that the Germans are certain to send their fleet round to attack the French Channel ports which we cannot permit. No, I fear there is no doubt. The halcyon days of peace are gone. All we can hope for is that honour will be quickly satisfied and the whole ghastly business won't last too many months."

"Anyhow, Marcus," he said more cheerfully, "I'm sure you and your men will be able to have a bit of a holiday in South-West Africa."

"I expect we will. But it raises the question of what is to become of young Humphrey here." Marcus had previously explained the Humphrey situation to Theo and Nicola so they understood his dilemma.

"I'm sure Theo could find something for Humphrey to do, couldn't you darling?" suggested Nicola.

"I'm sure I could," replied her spouse, "even if it was only temporary."

"That would rather defeat the purpose of him coming out here," objected Marcus. "The whole idea was for him to get some experience in setting up a business."

"Perhaps I should go home and enlist," suggested Humphrey.

"I think that's a rotten idea," said Marcus firmly. "As I said to you before, this war can't last long. By the time you've booked on a boat and arrived home, it'll probably be over and you'll have wasted all that time and effort."

"Well," suggested Humphrey, "suppose I sign up here. Perhaps I could join your unit. Then, when the war is over in a few months, we can go up to Rhodesia and do whatever it was we were going to do there."

"You know, Humphrey," said Marcus, "that's really not a bad idea at all. Have you had any military training?"
"I was in the cadets at school."

"Excellent!" said Marcus. "You can come down to the depot with me in the morning and meet my CO and we'll see what can be arranged." He supped his tea and beamed at the others. It looked as though the changes could be turned to good use after all.

CHAPTER EIGHT

MOLLY

Two things always stood out in Molly's mind afterwards when she thought of her time in the hospital near St Omer. The first was the smell. This was a combination of urine, disinfectant, faeces, and blood. When it rained, which it did quite a lot, the scent of damp earth was added to the cocktail, but the other elements always dominated. You were never free of it. It clung to your clothes so that even when you were away from the place back in your billet, it was still in your nostrils. You could bathe as thoroughly as you might, and change every article of clothing, but it was still there, a faint but unmistakable memento of the horrors to which you would soon have to return.

The second thing was the tiredness. Even when she came back on duty after a night's sleep, she felt tired to her bones. It wasn't just the physical fatigue from being on her feet all day and half the night, carrying heavy pans and buckets, helping to move beds and the bodies in them. It was also the unremitting mental strain of seeing those young bodies torn and battered, stumps roughly bandaged where a limb had been ripped off, gaping holes in the chest or abdomen exposing the organs within, the terrible wounds to the heads and faces. And, most heart-rending, the groans and cries of the men, most of them her age or younger, to whom these dreadful things had been done.

She did her best to seal her mind off from the sights she was obliged to see every day: you had to or it could not have been borne. Nothing in her life had prepared her, could possibly have prepared her, for what she experienced there in those tents and rough farm buildings where the base hospital had been set up. Molly had read the words of Florence Nightingale describing what she had seen in the hospital at Scutari, but these had not been able to convey the reality which now confronted Molly every day. What made it worse was that these battered and broken bodies belonged to people just like many she had known. They could have been her brothers' friends, lads from the village, men she had met at a party or a visit to York. For the first weeks she had lived in fear of having to treat someone she did actually know. Worst of all, she dreaded the day when she might look at some bandaged and bloodied figure lying on a stretcher below her and recognize Oliver. He at least was safe now, if only for the moment. A severe attack of dysentery had taken him out of the line and sent him back to England to recover, though she knew that it would only be a temporary respite. Much of the few precious days of leave from which she had just returned had been spent in his company. She knew that he had been thankful to be able to spend time with somebody who had some idea what it was really like out here. Not that they had talked about it very much at all, but their common experience gave a shared context to their lives which those who had not been there simply could not understand, however strong their love and empathy. Perhaps the war would end before Oliver had to plunge back into the maelstrom, but nobody now seemed to think that was likely. The old saying of "it'll all be over by Christmas" was a sick and sardonic joke to which the response now was "yes – but which year?"

Casualties brought in, especially on busy days when there had been a big 'stunt', as the soldiers called it, were roughly sorted into three categories to ensure that the overworked doctors and nurses were employed as effectively as possible. There were those whose injuries were such that they could wait for treatment. They were placed on one side. There were those for whom something could probably be done but who needed immediate attention. They were added to the queue and dealt with by the doctor or surgeon when they reached the head of it. And then there were the ones that were judged to be hopeless, on whom there was no point in wasting the precious medical resources. One of the doctors in Molly's first week, a very tall and thin Scot with a grey, deeply-lined face and battered black spectacles, had told her, "We just cannot treat them all. We must devote ourselves to the ones we can save. If we have time to look at these others, of course we will, but we must not be diverted. It's terrible to say it, but these men almost certainly have no hope. We must devote ourselves to those who have."

Molly remembered in particular one lad who had been brought in to the hospital soon after she started working there. The lower part of his body was wrapped in filthy and blood-soaked bandages, but his face, pale and drawn from pain and loss of blood, was quite unmarked. He looked about 18, and lay quietly, his eyes closed, hardly breathing. He was in the third category and was laid gently on the ground at the side of the tent. The orderly who had brought him in had pressed on her a crumpled and bloodied scrap of paper. "He give it me when we was bringing him in, miss, and asked if we could send it on to his mum. Do you think you can do that for him?"

Molly looked down at the paper and opened it. It was a letter, scrawled in pencil in a rounded, rather childish hand. "Dear Mum," it began. "I am well." She read no further. The lad had perhaps been writing it as he waited to go over the top and, rather than leaving it behind, had stuffed it into his pocket as the whistle sounded for him and his comrades to charge into the hell of no man's land. It was perhaps his last normal communication. She looked at his identity tag. '1144 W.R.Brown'. She scrawled it on the back of the letter and handed it to the hospital matron to see if it could be passed on. The matron, a small, dynamic professional nurse in her late forties, glanced up at Molly from the blood-stained missive in her hand. "Maybe better if she doesn't see this?

Don't worry, dear," she added after seeing Molly's expression. "I'll pass it on to the Colonel and he'll know what to do." The boy died a couple of hours later without regaining consciousness.

Molly's reverie was interrupted by the sound of wagon wheels and the cries of the orderlies telling her that a new batch of broken bodies had arrived. This was not unexpected. Although St Omer was sufficiently far behind the lines to be out of direct danger from shellfire, they could hear the guns as a distant rumble to the East, and a prolonged bombardment like the one they had been aware of over the past couple of days, invariably indicated a major attack, from one side or the other, with a consequent lift in the number of casualties requiring treatment.

Much later, sitting on her bed in the room she shared with two other nurses in a French family home on the outskirts of the town, she had a chance to think back on her recent precious days at home. Already they had an air of dreamlike unreality. The weather had not been very kind – grey, wet and cloudy most of the time – but the tranquil green beauty of the English countryside, with the cattle and sheep grazing peacefully as they always had, and the country folk going about their normal tasks had been a balm to Molly's soul. Had it not been for the men in uniform thronging the streets of York you might almost not have known there was a war on.

It was in York that she had an astonishing encounter that she had still not really come to terms with and which she again turned over in her mind. When she alighted from the London train, she had a couple of hours before she could board her connection to Cowdenhall, and she spent them just wandering around the beautiful old city, soaking up the blessed normality of life there, women doing their shopping or gossiping on the pavement, delivery boys on their bikes busily going about their business, carts and the occasional motor-car making their way down the street. Her wanderings took her to a part of York she had never been to before, a peaceful, narrow street of terraced houses. As she walked along the pavement, a young woman came into view, walking towards her, head down, pushing a pram. It wasn't until they were almost on each other that Molly realized with a shock that she knew her.

"Ruth!"

The woman lifted her head suddenly and flushed a deep red. She looked, Molly thought, tired, and her grey eyes, beneath the cowl of the cape she was wearing against the recent light drizzle, were troubled. She had not seen Ruth since before she left for France. Ruth had left Cowdenhall unexpectedly to go to York to nurse her sick aunt and, as far as she was aware, had not yet returned.

"Ruth! How lovely to see you! Is this where your aunt lives? And who is this?" She glanced down into the pram, occupied by a very small baby, fast asleep.

The girl didn't answer straightaway, but reached into the pram and touched the little cheek with her fingers. Then she seemed to make up her mind.

"She's the reason I'm here, Molly. The reason I had to come here."

"So it's your baby, Ruth?" All of a sudden she understood Ruth's sudden and mysterious disappearance from Cowdenhall a few weeks before Christmas.

"Gone to tend her aunt in York," Albert had explained to the Vicar. "She's right poorly and needs some looking after." It had seemed odd at the time, but now all was clear.

"Aye," said Ruth gently. "She's my bairn." She looked down at the sleeping baby. "I've called her Elizabeth, after my mam."

"And her father?" But as Molly asked the question she knew what the reply would be.

Ruth held her gaze steadily.

"I think you know," she said.

"Oh, Ruth! Does he know?"

"No!" said the girl urgently, "and you mustn't tell him! Please! Nobody knows except Dad and Emily and Aunt Mary." She laid her hand on Molly's arm. "Promise you won't tell him?"

"But Ruth, surely he has a right to know? You must tell him!"

"No!" said Ruth firmly. "Not now! Not yet! I can't have him worrying about it over there in Africa. It wouldn't be right. There's nowt he could do any road." She paused and fiddled with the button of her cape. "I will tell him, when he comes back, when this terrible war is over, but in the meanwhile, please promise you won't tell anybody?"

"All right, I promise. Not a word until you tell me."

"Oh, Molly! Thank you so!" Her voice broke and she squeezed Molly's arm tightly. "It weren't Humphrey's fault, you know. It were all me. I made him love me."

Molly smiled wryly. "Well, I'm sure he didn't need a lot of persuading. Can I see where you live?"

The two girls walked together back down the road to Aunt Mary's house, a neat little place with a polished door knob and a spotless front step. As they entered, baby Elizabeth awoke and let them know that she expected to be fed, so they settled in the front parlour while Ruth unselfconsciously held the little creature to her bosom. Molly had hitherto had very little to do with small babies, and marveled at the soft, pink perfection of her tiny hands and the creased concentration of her little face as she sucked strongly on her mother's soft white breast.

There was no sign of the aunt. "She's got a job," explained Ruth, "down at the haberdashers, helping out behind the counter. One good thing about this awful war is, with all the lads joining up, there's many more jobs for women." Molly learned that Aunt Mary was a widow whose husband had died in a factory accident when she was quite young. She had never married again. "I reckon she were too independent," said Ruth with a laugh. "Couldn't find any man she were ready to have under her feet or telling her what to do." Times had been hard in the early years, and Mary had done a lot of washing and scrubbing floors, but she'd survived and managed to hold onto their dwelling. She had one son, Edward, aged just 15, who was lucky enough to have a job as a paperboy. "He wants to join up," said Ruth, "but he's far too young and

Mary'll never let him. She says only a buffle-head would sign up for that. Happen it'll be all over by the time he's old enough to go."

"What can I do to help," said Molly.

"Nothing!" said Ruth firmly. "We've got all we need. Dad wants us to give her away – you know, put her for adoption. But I won't! She's part of me!" and she added softly, "part of Humphrey."

Molly felt her heart go out to the girl. "Has your father seen her?"

"No. And he says I can't come home 'til she's gone." She smiled wryly. "So I reckon I won't be seeing your folks. Lucky I've got Aunt Mary on my side."

§

Molly had to leave soon after to catch her train. The girls exchanged a warm embrace and Molly once more had to promise faithfully to keep Elizabeth a secret for the time being. As she walked slowly along the streets of the old city to the station, her brain was seething with possibilities and impossibilities. What would Humphrey think, if he knew? And what would he do? How was she going to stop herself telling her family? How was she to be civil to Albert Moffat if they should happen to meet? Illegitimate births were a terrible scandal in a small community, she could understand that. But – to cut off your own daughter? Molly had not formed a very good opinion of the male sex outside her own family, and this did nothing to improve it. It was going to be a difficult time. She thought again of Humphrey, thousands of miles away across the sea in a strange and savage land. He deserved to know something as important as this, and she made up her mind to do everything she could to convince Ruth of that.

CORRESPONDENCE – 3

Mrs Louisa Nayland
The Vicarage
Cowdenhall
Yorkshire

June 1915

Dearest Mother

Thank you so much for the letters which I got when I arrived at the hospital here two days ago. Postal deliveries are a bit difficult when we are out in the bush!

I wanted to write to you straightaway after I was wounded to let you know I was alright, but Marcus insisted that he would, which was very decent of him. You mustn't worry about me. As I expect Marcus told you, it was a very little wound – just bad luck really - a stray bullet whizzing around went through my arm, and I probably wouldn't have had to go back out of the line except it got infected and I was a bit poorly for a few days which is why they sent me to the hospital here. I'm feeling so much better now, just the arm a bit sore, and I hope I will be able to get back to the unit before too long.

We have been doing so well. I can't say too much or the officers who check our mail will start scrubbing things out! I think the Germans are on the run though, and it won't be too long before they give up. We hadn't seen any for several days before the skirmish when I got my wound. The other lads in the unit are real pals – it's like being part of a rugger team at school and we all help each other out. The special friend I told you about in my last letter, Koos (I think that's how you spell his name – I had to ask him!) was wonderful when I got shot and helped me back to the dressing station and carried my kit.

I must say it's quite nice to be back in civilization for a bit and sleep in a proper bed. You do get used to curling up on a groundsheet under a bush but it's still not very restful and the food is far from exciting – mostly tinned meat and vegetables and some amazingly hard biscuits which I suppose must be good for you. I'm afraid you wouldn't think much of the hygiene arrangements out there, either. Water is very scarce so we can't afford to use much for washing, let alone bathing. Once when we came to quite a wide river which we had to cross with rafts and canoes, it was wonderful to see how everybody tore off their clothes and splashed around in the shallows. The old hands said we had to look out for crocodiles but I didn't see any!

It's quite jolly here in the hospital. There aren't very many of us – I think most of the wounded get sent back to Cape Town – and none of us is too ill so you can chat and wander around the hospital grounds. I haven't yet been able to go into town so I can't tell you what Bloemfontein is like, but I hope they will let me out tomorrow or the day after. Some of the chaps have been able to go and stay with local people here, which would be fun. The soldier in the next bed to me is also English, a very nice chap called Peter Merry who lives near Petworth in Sussex. He came out to South Africa to work for his uncle on a farm close to Durban and joined up when the war started. He's just about fully fit now so I expect he'll be going out soon.

The nurses are ever so kind and can't do enough for you. Most of them are Dutch, though, and don't speak English very well. Koos did teach me a few words of Afrikaans (that's the language the Dutch people speak out here) but I'm afraid they haven't been much use to me in hospital. There isn't much call to say "Watch out! Enemy sniper in that tree!" or "Can I share your mess tin?"

Please do write again and give me all the news. I suppose Oliver will be going back to the front now he is recovered from his illness. I expect you will be anxious about him, but I'm sure he'll be fine – you know Ollie! He's indestructible! I wonder how Moll is getting on in France? You know, I wasn't at all surprised to hear she had joined up. She'll make a terrific nurse, just the sort of person a chap needs to look after him when he is laid low. I think I know that better than anybody!

Does father ever speak to Albert Moffat? I had several letters

87

from Ruth before Christmas but haven't heard from her for months. I hope nothing's wrong.

Do give my love to everybody, not forgetting Dizzy. One of the doctors here has a little terrier who reminds me of Dizzy. He's not supposed to go into the hospital rooms but he often escapes and finds his way in and we all make a great fuss of him and feed him scraps until one of the staff finds him and shoos him out!

With much love

Humphrey

British Military Hospital no.3
Bloemfontein

CHAPTER NINE

TIENEKE

July nights in the Free State are cold. As Tieneke Vermuelen stepped off the stoep of the farmhouse to go to the water-tank with her bucket, the grass scrunched beneath her feet with the frost. Behind the tank the sun was just about to appear above the horizon, and the barn and the tank showed as black silhouettes against the red and yellow glow of the dawn. Behind her in the kitchen she could hear the banging and clattering of her son, Johannes, and the kitchen boy stoking up the fire in the oven to provide some warmth and to cook their breakfast.

Tieneke was a slim but strongly-built woman, a year or two short of her fortieth birthday. She was a little over medium height and wore her blonde hair tied back from her face which, like her arms, was deeply tanned from years of exposure to a harsh environment.

"No wonder the kaffirs are so black," her neighbor Cobus had once remarked jocularly. "They've been standing around under this sun for thousands of years! If we stay here long enough, we'll all end up looking the same!"

Her face had been strikingly pretty when she was a girl and remained handsome, with high cheek bones and a full, sensuous mouth. But the years had etched lines and wrinkles around the mouth and eyes that bore witness to many days spent outdoors in all weathers and hard times endured. Tieneke's life had never been easy. A farmer's daughter, she had been little more than a girl when she married Oskar Vermuelen and went to live with him on his farm a day's trek from Bloemfontein.

The outbreak of the second Boer War between the British Government and the Dutch farmers' republics had found her, a young woman with two very small children, in sole charge of a busy farm with several hundred acres under wheat and maize, as well as cattle and poultry, and a workforce of dozens. As it had become clear that negotiations between the British and the Boer republics were going nowhere and that war was inevitable, Oskar had seized his rifle, mounted his horse and taken off to join the rebels. He had spent the next three years leading a commando under General Botha. When hostilities ended in a Boer defeat, some were able to swallow the bitter pill of assimilation and accept a new life as part of the British Empire. Botha himself, indeed, was now the Prime Minister of the Union of South Africa. Many though, like Oskar, had been unwilling to accept the humiliations placed on them by the Treaty of Vereeniging and instead chose exile, first in the neighbouring Portuguese colony of Mozambique and then back in Holland, whence his forebears had emigrated many generations before.

Tieneke remembered with great clarity the day when the British soldiers had arrived at the farm, ostensibly looking for Oskar. Naturally they found no sign of him, but they firmly seized Tieneke and her children and took them away in an ox-cart, with what possessions they were able to carry with them. Eventually they had ended up in one of the camps that had been set up for such internees – the notorious 'concentration camps'. The one that became their home for the next two and a half years was at Harrismith, far to the east near the border with Natal. Their guardians in the camp were not especially unkind or unsympathetic, but conditions were appalling. Gross overcrowding, totally inadequate sanitary facilities and low standards of hygiene, meant that diseases of all sorts sprang up and flourished – measles, typhoid, and dysentery were endemic.

It was the last of these afflictions that claimed the life of four-year-old Marianna Vermuelen. Her little body, already weakened by months of malnutrition, had given up the struggle, and she died in her mother's arms.

It would not have been surprising if these experiences had left Tieneke with a deep and abiding hatred of the 'Rooineks' but, curiously, they had not. Perhaps this was partly because of her English grandmother, a family antecedent which had subjected her to a great deal of unkind teasing when she was a child. She had nothing but contempt for the leaders who had set the camps up, for the generals and ministers who believed that imposing this sort of misery on their fellow human beings was an acceptable way to win a war. But she knew that the bulk of the British people were ordinary, decent folk, who had not been consulted on the policy and would probably not have agreed to it if they had been. She knew this from those she had met. One of these was a nurse, an Englishwoman, one of the very few able to work in the camp, who had also been at the side of the rough cot in the tent at Harrismith the night her daughter had given up the struggle to survive. She had wept and held Tieneke's hands tightly in her own saying, over and over again, "I'm so sorry! I'm so sorry." Tieneke herself had remained dry-eyed while they wrapped the little body in a blanket and took her down to the end of the camp enclosure where she was laid in a pit with two others who had died that day. It was only later that night as she lay on her own cot and could tell, from his regular breathing, that Johannes was asleep, that she broke and allowed herself the luxury of bitter tears of sadness and regret for a life snuffed out so pitiably short.

When the war ended, she grasped her little son by the hand and made her way back to the farm, getting rides on farm carts and, one wonderful journey, a motorcar, which left Johannes round-eyed and speechless with awe and delight.

The farm had been laid waste – crops destroyed or expropriated, livestock butchered or driven off. What the soldiers left behind had been pillaged by the baboons or the remaining African workers. Some of these had been rounded up and placed in their own camps where, she had heard, conditions were even worse than in the camps for whites. Many, though, had escaped capture, taking to their heels and hiding when they saw the troops approach, and a few of these returned when they heard that the owner was back. One such, thankfully, was the Headman, Carl, a leathery, wrinkled Sotho, who had worked on the property from a boy. He was still with her, all these years later, though now getting old and even more lined and leathery. She knew she could never possibly have restored the farm to a working unit without him. His depth of knowledge, his common sense, his determination, which matched her own, to see the farm producing again, meant that within a surprisingly short time, it did. Now it provided her and Johannes with a good livelihood, albeit at the cost of considerable hard work and dedication. Carl had been her rock, as well as motivating and organizing the African farm workers in a way that she could never have managed. She knew her debt to him was immense.

When Tieneke returned to the kitchen, the range was blazing and the mealie porridge for their breakfast was cooking up.

"Now, Hannes, you've remembered I'm going in to Bloemfontein today, so you'll be in charge." Her son was a strongly built young man of nineteen, with his father's beaky nose and square jaw and his mother's piercing blue eyes and blond hair.

"Yes, Ma. Don't worry! I can handle it!" They spoke their native tongue, Afrikaans.

There was a respectful tap at the door. Carl was standing there, the blanket wrapped around his shoulders contrasting oddly with his bare legs, the extremities of which were encased in rough, home-made sandals.

"Good morning, Carl."

"Good morning, missus." They too spoke in Afrikaans, although Tieneke was fluent in Carl's tongue, Sotho, in which they would sometimes converse in more relaxed circumstances. Afrikaans was the language of the work-place!

"Did you catch me those chickens for the hospital?"

"Yes, missus, they are in the back of the cart."

"And Lesebo?"

"He too is ready in the cart, missus."

"Good. I should be back tomorrow evening. Baas Hannes is in charge while I am away. You know what to do."

"Yes, missus." The old man smiled and nodded his head. "Go well!"

§

The farm was not a long distance from Bloemfontein but, with the ox-cart travelling at little more than walking pace, it was a good day's journey. On a horse, of course, it could be done much faster.

Tieneke remembered as if it were last week that day several years before when Hannes, just a boy, had been bitten by a puff-adder. This stout and sluggish snake is responsible for more snakebites than any other species in Africa, not because it is particularly aggressive but because its torpid nature makes it far more likely to be trodden on by unwary human feet. When Hannes came running in crying from the rocky kopje behind the homestead, Tieneke knew that, without any means of treatment on her own or neighbouring farms, his only hope of salvation was to transport the lad to the hospital in Bloemfontein. There they might have supplies of the new anti-venene. She caught and saddled the horse in minutes, swung the frightened child up in front of her on the saddle, and set out. They made it in just under three hours. As they neared their destination, the boy started to slip in and out of consciousness and Tieneke had to hang onto him round the waist with one hand while gripping the reins in the other. By the time they pulled up outside the hospital building, her arms were numb and aching and hardly able to assist the willing hands that helped her and the unconscious Johannes down from their mount and carried the boy inside. The mare was completely spent and simply stood in the courtyard, her head down, soaked with sweat, her flanks heaving and flesh twitching.

The Englishman in charge of the hospital at the time, Dr Padbury, had taken over the case immediately, and Tieneke had no doubt that her son owed his life and his complete recovery to Padbury's calm competence and meticulous attention to detail on that day and later when Johannes' life still hung in the balance. Her gratitude showed itself in gifts of farm produce when she had occasion to come to town. Dr Padbury himself had moved on, but several of the nursing staff from that time remained, so she often still brought in something, vegetables, fresh mealies in the season, a couple of chickens or some eggs.

This day she pulled up more decorously in the courtyard of the hospital, and waited while Lesebo, the lad who had accompanied her, took the chickens round to the kitchen. The three birds, tied together by their legs, wriggled and squawked in agitation, unaware of the fate that awaited them but doubtless suspecting that bad things lay ahead.

While she was waiting for Lesebo to return, Tieneke led the ox to the large trough in the courtyard where the animal gratefully slaked its thirst. As he did, she glanced up and saw a young English soldier standing there.

"Gooie more, mevrou," he said, in heavily accented Afrikaans.

"Good morning, English," she replied in his own tongue.

"I'm sorry!" He smiled wrily. "I'm afraid my Afrikaans is not very good. I have a Dutch pal in my unit who has taught me just a few words." He was a little taller than her, with a pleasant open face, blue eyes, and sandy hair cut short in the military style. He wore a smart uniform with insignia that were unfamiliar to Tieneke and his left arm was carried in a black sling. He looked little older than Hannes.

"You hurt your arm?" She gestured to his sling.

"Oh, it's fine now." He laughed. "I think they make me wear this to remind me I'm a patient. I should be out of here in a few days."

94

At that moment the matron, Sister Hannaford, appeared at the front door.

"Thank you for the chickens, Mevrou Vermuelen. They are very welcome. Let me pay you for them." This was a charade that was played out every time Tieneke brought something to the hospital. Very occasionally, when she was particularly short of cash, she would accept some payment. Not today.

"Thank you, Sister, that is not necessary. It is my pleasure." During this conversation Lesebo had reappeared and hopped into the cart, so Tieneke resumed her seat on the bench at the front of it.

"Good day, Sister." She smiled at the young soldier. "Good day, English."

§

Tieneke spent the night, as she usually did on her visits to Bloemfontein, with her friend Ilsa Potgieter, a widow who ran a small boarding house on the outskirts of town. The ox was turned out into the small paddock behind the house, and Lesebo slept in one of the huts of Ilsa's servants nearby. The next morning she went into town to collect the various things she needed to take back to the farm. As she came out of the hardware store, she almost bumped into the young soldier she had seen at the hospital the evening before. He was dressed much as he had been then, except that the sling had been discarded. He smiled at her.

"Mrs Vermeulen! Fancy seeing you again!"

"You have a good memory, English!" She looked at his friendly, youthful, face. A sudden impulse took hold of her, and before she had a chance to think about it, she heard herself say, "Would you like to spend some days at our farm?"

The young man was evidently somewhat taken aback. "Why… yes, that would be very nice. Will your husband want me there?"

"I do not have a husband, English, just my son, Hannes. He is about the same age as you. He will be happy to look after you."

"Well, if you're sure. I'd love to. I'd need to clear it with the hospital staff, but I'm sure they won't mind. I can only stay for a few days, though."

"Good!" she said. "I can send you back with one of the boys on a horse. You can ride a horse?"

He laughed. "Yes. I can ride a horse."

"So, go back to the hospital and do what is needed, and we will pick you up on our way out. In about one hour?"

"I'll be there!" He turned and hastened away.

"Wait!" said Tieneke. "What's your name?" The boy stopped and turned.

"Humphrey. Humphrey Nayland." He grinned. " Trooper Nayland 986583." He turned and went off.

Tieneke's brain whirled. Am I mad? She asked herself. What am I thinking of? Lesebo had watched, with interest though little understanding, these proceedings from his perch on the back of the cart.

"Is the English baas coming with us, Missus?" he enquired.

"None of your business!" she retorted. "Now, we must finish our buying!"

§

He was waiting near the entry to the hospital when the wagon got there, his kitbag slung over his shoulder. He wedged it safely on the wagon and then climbed up on the bench at the front next to Tieneke.

"So, they have let you come?" she said with a sideways glance.

Humphrey laughed. "To be honest, I think they're glad to be rid of us! I will have to be back by Thursday, though." It was Monday. "The chief doctor is due back from Cape Town and the nurse thinks he will want to examine me so that they can send me back to my unit. You speak English very well, Mrs Vermeulen."

"I learned it in the camp during the war – the last war between us and you English. I have kept on speaking it. It can be useful. Don't worry," she went on with a smile, seeing the doubtful look that passed across his face, "I'm not a spy. I do not like the Germans. And you should call me by my name. It is Tieneke. Mrs Vermeulen makes me sound like an old woman!"

The boy laughed. "Alright – Tieneke!" They travelled on in silence for a while.

"So, tell me, Ham …."

"Humphrey!"

"Humphrey, what is your family back home in England?"

"Well, my father is a clergyman, and we live in a village called Cowdenhall in Yorkshire in the north of England. I have two sisters and a brother, all older than me. My older sister is married to a Canadian and they usually live in Canada. My other sister is a nurse. I think she is in France at the moment."

"And your brother?"

"He is a soldier too. A real one – he was in the army before the war. I'm not sure where he is. He got very sick and had to go home to England, but I expect they will send him back to the Front when he is well."

"And do you have a ... liefling ... how do you say? ... a sweet one ... a sweetheart?"

Humphrey didn't answer straight away. "There is a girl I was fond of," he said quietly, "but I haven't heard from her for many months." They rode on in silence for a while.

§

It was late afternoon by the time the ox plodded up the track leading to the farmhouse. Hannes greeted them while two of the servants unloaded the various goods from the back of the cart. He stared suspiciously at Humphrey.

"Who is this, Ma? What is he doing here?"

"His name is Humphrey. He is an English soldier from the hospital who has come to stay with us for a few days?"

"Why?"

"Because I invited him. You will welcome him. He is our

guest." She turned to Humphrey and said, in English, "This is my son, Hannes. He will look after you. He does not speak English very much but I am sure you will understand each other."

Humphrey climber rather stiffly down from the bench and held out his hand. After a moment's hesitation, Hannes shook it. "Welkom," he said, unenthusiastically.

Tieneke supervised the unloading of the cart.

"Hannes," she said, "take the English, his name is Humphrey, up to the kopje and show him the farm. I will speak to Carl to find out what has happened while I was away." The old headman had just appeared and they greeted each other while the two young men walked away towards the kopje.

"Is it well, Carl?"

"One of the new calves has disappeared, missus."

"Disappeared? What do you mean?"

"I think a leopard has taken it. There was blood and I could see its spoor. Baas Hannes and I followed it for a while but we lost the track."

"That is not good, Carl. We must keep a sharp look out. It might be necessary to try and shoot it."

Carl nodded. "I think so, missus. Teboho lost a goat a week ago and he thought it was the same leopard." The occasional depredation by wild animals was a fact of life, though a good deal less frequent now than it had been in the early days of the farm. The last serious incident had been some eight years before when a rather elderly lion, presumably an outcast from his pride, had wandered onto the farm and helped himself to several of the domestic livestock before Tieneke and Carl had tracked him down and a bullet from her old Mauser rifle had brought his career to an end. Hannes, then only a young boy, had been furious that his mother had refused to let him accompany her on the hunt. However, he had rejoiced at the success of the enterprise, had watched while the animal was skinned and its hide pegged out to dry, and claimed one of the claws as a trophy which he now wore on a leather thong around his neck for good luck.

By the time Hannes and Humphrey had returned from their tour, Tieneke was comfortably ensconced in her chair on the stoep, enjoying a cool glass of water.

"You have a wonderful farm here, Tieneke!" said Humphrey enthusiastically. His face was flushed from his exertions, though he had kept his jacket on. There was already an evening chill in the air. He spread out his arms. "So big!"

Tieneke laughed. "Not so big," she said. "Many other farmers here have farms that are bigger. But it is enough for us. Hannes, show Humphrey where he is to sleep and where he can wash before we have supper."

§

After they had eaten they returned to the stoep and sat on the chairs looking out. The sun had long gone down and the moon was not yet up, so it was a dark night, lit up only by the myriad stars that twinkled like tiny sequins in the black velvet canopy of the sky. There was a pronounced drop in temperature and Tieneke had wrapped a shawl around her shoulders. She had brought a bottle with her from the cupboard with three glasses and she splashed a measure of the liquid into each.

"What is it?" said Humphrey, sniffing the glass curiously.

"It is a spirit. Made from appelkoos."

"Apple?"

"No. Different fruit. You call it … abricot, apricot?"

Humphrey took a tentative sip and then a mouthful while she watched him with amusement. The light from the lantern which hung from the beam above them threw shadows across his face and a glint in his eyes.

"It is very good!" he pronounced. "Quite sweet."

"Ja, it is good." She leaned forward and filled his glass up. "Tell me more about life in England. Does it rain much? Do you ever get snow?"

Humphrey told her about Yorkshire, the countryside and the

people. He talked about his experiences at school and some of the escapades that he and Molly had got up to.

Hannes abandoned them fairly early on. Bored at sitting listening to a conversation he barely understood, he finished his drink and went off, rather grumpily, to bed.

"What about you, Tieneke? What was it like when you were a little girl?"

So she told him about growing up on her parents' farm, about meeting Oskar, and the early days on their property. And then the Boer War.

"And where is your husband now?" he asked.

"I don't know. I heard he went back to Holland. All his people have died or moved away, so there is nobody to tell me. My neighbor Cobus said there was a rumour he had gone to one of the German colonies, in East Africa, but I don't know if that is true."

Humphrey was appalled to hear about the camp at Harrismith.

"But that is terrible, Tieneke! I never knew that sort of thing happened!"

"I think your government did not wish you to know!"

"You must hate us" he said.

"No, not hate. Sadness, but not hate. Hate is not good. It can fill you up and leave no room for anything else." She looked across at him. The bottle on the table between them was nearly empty. The moon had started to rise and its beams compensated for the failing light of the lantern which had started to gutter and die.

"Come and sit here, English." She indicated the chair next to her that Hannes had vacated. Humphrey came across and sat there. Their arms were almost touching. She could sense a tension in his body. She turned to face him and put her hand on his arm. She could feel it trembling slightly.

"Have you ever loved a girl, Humphrey?" He lifted his face to look at her. His eyes were wide and his face, in the moonlight, seemed pale, almost ghostly.

"Yes … I … once… I did." His voice was broken and uncertain.

Tieneke stood up and pulled him to his feet. They stood very close. She looked up and kissed him, gently but with increasing urgency. His lips were warm and tasted of apricot brandy. His arms drew her close, hesitantly to begin with and then with strength and passion. She could feel the swelling of his body against her legs. They disengaged and she took his hand.

"Come, English." She turned and led him down the stoep towards her room. The moonlight through the window helped them see as they took off their clothes until they stood beside her bed, naked. She ran her hand down from his waist between his legs, and heard him gasp suddenly as she touched him. She could feel his whole body trembling and he pulled her face towards him. After a while she disengaged and lay on the bed, pulling him down towards her.

"Come into me, English," she murmured huskily, and lay back so that he could.

§

Afterwards Tieneke got up and washed at the basin and then returned to the bed, wrapping herself in a blanket for warmth. Humphrey was on his side facing away from her, still and silent. She felt content and at peace. Humphrey may have lacked the practiced expertise of an experienced lover, but the intensity of his passion had matched hers and this, combined with a consideration and gentleness that she had not expected, had been deeply satisfying. It had been quite a long time for her. Over the years the needs of her body had driven her, from time to time, to slake that particular thirst. However, she had never been tempted to form any sort of permanent attachment. Apart from the fact that she was still, legally, a married woman, she had become too used to, and protective of, her independence to want to give it up again. She neither wanted nor needed a man getting under her feet or, worse, giving her orders, telling her what she may or may not do. Hannes and, to a lesser extent, Carl and the other farm workers, satisfied her need for human companionship. She had come to realize that, most of the time, she preferred her own company. Perhaps it was selfish, she thought, but it was good not to have to consider the intimate needs of anyone but herself.

She glanced over at the inert form beside her and laid her hand on his waist.

"Humphrey?" she said softly. There was no reply. She could tell he was not asleep.

"Humphrey? "she repeated, "are you all right?" He nodded wordlessly. She gripped his shoulder and tugged.

"Humphrey! Look at me!" Slowly he turned over to face her. His face was indistinct in the darkness, but she caught a glimpse of moisture on his cheek.

"What is it?" she cried. "What is the matter?"

"I … I have betrayed her," he said softly.

"Betrayed who?"

"Ruth … my girl at home."

"But I thought you did not have any word from her?"

"I didn't. But I am sure something must have prevented her. I know it would not be her fault." He looked down and traced a pattern on the sheet with his finger. "When we left, I promised I would love her forever, that I would come back to her. And now this …" He gestured about him with his hand.

Tieneke regarded him in silence for a few seconds, and then reached forward and grasped his hand.

"Listen to me, Humphrey! What we have done tonight was lekker, it was very good, it was …." she searched for the words, " a beautiful accident! I do not expect anything from you, you must not expect anything from me! After all," she added with a laugh, "I am nearly old enough to be your mother. When this war is finished, you will go home, and you will marry your girl, and you will be happy together. I will just be a memory from the past – I hope a good one!"

Humphrey seemed to consider this. "I hope you are right," he said at last. "But we mustn't … we mustn't do this again."

"No," she agreed. "We will not do it again. But," she lifted her hand and brushed his cheek gently, "do not be sad. It was lekker, eh? Now go!" She watched from the bed as Humphrey dressed.

"What do we say to Hannes?" he asked.

"We say nothing," she replied firmly. "Hannes is not a fool. He will know something has happened. He knows I am not like a non in a klooster. But he will not ask, and we will not tell. That way we will all be more happy."

When he was finished she got up from the bed, wrapped in her blanket, and walked with him to the door out onto the stoep. When they got there she looked up into his eyes and smiled. She reached up on her tip toes and kissed him gently on the lips. Then she placed the palm of her hand on his chest and pushed him away.

"Now go, English. Sleep well!" She closed the door behind him and went back to bed.

§

For the next two days Tieneke was able to immerse herself in the work of the farm and so sublimate any desires that might have weakened her resolution. There were times when she glanced at Humphrey across the table at meals, or watched him making friends with one of the farm dogs, and the memory of his strong young body came flooding back, but she was able to suppress it. She knew that what she had said to him that night was right. There was no future together for them and it would have been very foolish to pretend there was.

The first day she sent him off with Hannes and one of the farm boys with the rifle to see if they could track down the leopard. They were gone nearly the whole day and when they returned in the late afternoon she was glad to sense a lessening of the tension that there had been between the two young men. They were walking along side by side and Hannes seemed much more cheerful than when they had left. The farm boy, Matthias, was following behind with some animal's body on his shoulders.

"No sign of the tiger, Ma," said Hannes. Like many, he used the same Afrikaans word 'tier' for tiger and leopard. "Matthias thinks the animal heard you were back and moved onto Cobus' farm. We got a duiker, though. Humphrey shot it."

"Did you, Humphrey? That was well done!"

"It wasn't hard. He was quite close, poor little thing." He laughed. "Perhaps my army training will be useful after all. I think it's the first thing I've ever shot."

"What? No Germans?"

Humphrey grinned. "I don't think so. I've hardly even seen any, apart from those who surrendered to us."

They had a leg of the hapless little antelope for dinner that night. It was tasty though a bit tough. "It will be better," said Tieneke, "when we have hung it in the larder for a few days. Hannes will make some biltong also."

§

Quite a little farewell committee gathered early in the morning two days later to see Humphrey off – Carl and Matthias as well as Tieneke and Hannes. Lesebo was mounted on the spare pony. He would bring both horses back once Humphrey had been delivered to the hospital. Humphrey shook hands with the two Africans and then with Hannes.

"Thank you for your kindness" he said.

"Totsiens, man," said Hannes. "Go well!"

Tieneke watched as Humphrey swung into the saddle and secured his kitbag behind him. She had a strange feeling of unreality. Less than four days ago she had never set eyes on this boy. Now he was again passing out of her life for ever, but in between he had become a small part of her and, she wanted to think, she of him.

"Travel carefully, English," she said. "Do not forget us."

"Thank you, Tieneke. Thank you for everything." He looked straight at her. "I will never forget you." He held her gaze for a long moment, as though waiting to say something else, and then turned his horse's head and trotted off down the track, with Lesebo following. Tieneke felt a cold hand on her heart. She watched for a few seconds as the riders moved away, and then turned abruptly and went up the stairs into the farmhouse.

CORRESPONDENCE – 4

Lieut.Humphrey Nayland
On service with Rhodesia Native Regiment
Salisbury
Rhodesia

March 1916

My dearest Piglet

It was so wonderful to get your lovely long letter which Mother sent on to me. I'm sorry it has taken such a long time for me to reply but we've been so busy that I haven't had a moment to myself. At last I've been lucky enough to get a couple of days' leave and one of the other nurses and me have escaped to a little boarding house in Boulogne.

The accommodation is a bit cramped – my friend Joan and I have two little beds almost touching in the same tiny room and one wardrobe between us. As she says, 'you couldn't swing a cat in here' (why would you want to? I LOVE cats!). But we don't have to get up 'til we feel like it and when we do we only have to worry about where we're going for lunch and what to wear (not a lot of choice there, as you can imagine!). Madame is rather cranky and claims to speak NO English at all (I bet she does but pretends she doesn't just to be difficult). Her cooking's quite good though and she is happy to leave us alone. It is just bliss!

What it means, of course, my dear Piglet, is that I can now give your letter the attention it deserves! What good news about your promotion! Or at least I suppose it is. Joan says the officers always get killed first but she is a bit of a gloompot. Do they pay you more, and is the food any better? I am intrigued to know more about your new regiment. The name (Rhodesia NATIVE Regiment) seems to say that they are all blacks. Is that right? Do they speak English or are you going to have to learn their language? I was so glad to hear that your friend Koos (did I get that right?) has also moved with you. Having friends with you makes the worst things bearable. I suppose Marcus, being a bit more senior, had to stay.

I expect Mother has told you that Ollie is now back at the Front. He and I were able to spend a couple of days together at home when I was on leave which was lovely. He was very thin (dysentery does that to you!) but otherwise quite fit and seemed cheerful enough. I suspect he was putting on a brave face though. So many of his friends have gone. Even Col Fortescue. Ollie said a great shell landed on battalion HQ and all the officers around the colonel were blown to pieces. It was a miracle he survived, although he had quite severe wounds and is apparently now as deaf as a post. As Ollie says. 'He's a tough old so-and-so! It'll take more than the Germans to get him!' I expect his war is over, though.

Did mother tell you about Ollie's promotion to major? It came through just before he went back to the Front, so they were able to have a bit of a celebration. I am sure that he and Mary Elizabeth were right to get married before he went to Belgium, though it was sad that you and Gertie couldn't be there. M E is still living with her parents and Ollie stays there when he is home. I think that she and Edith come round to the Vicarage a lot and I'm sure that they and mother give each other support. It really helps if you have somebody there who has the same cares and worries that you do!

As for me, I soldier on as Nanny Elliot used to tell us we had to do! It does get depressing at times – there's often so little we can do for these poor boys who come to us except make them comfortable and give them something for the pain (if we haven't run out of morphine which often happens!) Joan says that if the last thing some poor soldier sees is my smiling face then he'll die happy and that's better than nothing. I suppose she might be right! Full of homespun wisdom, our Joan!

I'm sitting in a deck chair writing this by the beach at Boulogne, and if you looked straight ahead you might not know there was a war on. By the water's edge there's a little boy and his dad, I suppose, flying a kite. The wind is quite strong and gusty so the kite's flying jolly well and you can tell that the little boy is having so much fun. But it's all an illusion. If you look down the beach towards the harbour you can see the warships at anchor there and when I turn round to the prom behind me there are lots of soldiers and other uniforms walking up and down there. We're a long way from the front line here but still, when the wind is blowing in the right direction, you can hear that faint rumble in the distance that is the guns. It's hard to believe that just two years ago we were sitting having tea and scones in the garden and the worst things that happened were a fox getting into the chicken-run or father losing the notes for his sermon!

It looks like there is a bit of a squall on the way from the Channel so I'd better pack up my troubles, as they say. I don't want to get wet! There is just one other thing I must say, and I've left it to the last. When I was at home I met Ruth in York. It is the second time I've seen her – the first was just by chance, but this time I sought her out. She is quite well and I am sure she feels the same about you as she ever did. That is all I'm allowed to say! When you come back you will see her and find out everything for yourself. There! Oh! Rain!

Later: I misjudged the squall and would have got very wet indeed if not for a young Canadian soldier who very kindly lent me his cape. I asked him if he had heard of the Empire of the Lord and he obviously had no idea what I was talking about! I'm afraid Gertie and Mackenzie have got some work to do on the home front!

I'd better finish this now so I can get it in the post before Joan and I have to go back up the road tomorrow morning. Please, dear Piglet, look after yourself! As I think you know, I'm not a great one for prayer (a sad disappointment to Father!) but even so I say a prayer for you every morning when I wake up and every night before I sleep. So if there IS a God, you jolly well should be alright! Give my best wishes to your friends, even though I have never met them, and perhaps my love to Marcus if you see him (or perhaps not – I don't want him getting the wrong impression! Still we're all so far apart it probably doesn't matter!)

This comes with all my love and a big hug
Your devoted sister

Molly
Advanced Base Hospital
St Omer (actually Chez Fournier, 2 Avenue Le Grec, Boulogne-sur-mer!)

CHAPTER TEN

KOOS

Koos van Rensburg had spent virtually all his life in the African bush. Born and raised on his family's farm near Marandellas, south-east of Salisbury, some of his earliest memories were of accompanying his father or one of the African farm-workers on little hunting forays into the woodland and forests adjacent to the farm. When he was old enough to own his own rifle he had occasionally stayed out overnight, camping in a bivouac under a musasa tree and making a fire to roast a guinea-fowl or hare if he been lucky enough to bag one. However, he freely acknowledged that this had not prepared him for the war in the jungles of German East Africa.

For one thing, the weather was much more severe. It seemed to him that since the start of the campaign they had endured almost endless rain, which turned the black-cotton soil of the paths into a sludgy quagmire that made walking on the flat, let alone up steep hills, an exhausting torture. It was impossible to keep anything dry, and wet clothing, not changed sometimes for weeks on end, soon stank and caused painful chafing. When the rain did clear, it was replaced by energy-sapping heat that wrung the sweat out of your body and made progress through the still muddy tracks even more of a trial.

The terrain and the topography added fresh challenges. In the southern highlands where they now were, they had to traverse steep valleys, heavily wooded, often with considerable rivers flowing between them which sometimes required the laborious construction of crude bridges to enable the passage of guns and stores. Where the ground was flatter it was often covered in elephant grass six or seven feet high, so thick that you might pass five paces away from a man and be quite unaware he was there. You could never be sure whether the rustling a few feet away was something harmless like a bush-buck or a duiker, a potentially fatal threat such as a buffalo, or an even more certainly menacing patrol of German *askaris* (soldiers).

One of the major consequences of the condition of the tracks – you could hardly call them roads – was that supply was a nightmare. Even if there had been sufficient motor vehicles, and Koos suspected there were not (he had certainly hardly seen any) they were quite unable to move on any but the very few main trunk routes and, when the rains were heavy, not far on those either. Reliance early in the war on beasts of burden – horses, oxen, mules – had failed to solve the problem because of the prevalence in the area of the tsetse fly. Sleeping sickness, the deadly parasite carried by this disagreeable little insect, was invariably fatal to domestic livestock and made reliance on them impossible. The consequence of all of this was that, by the time Koos and his fellow-warriors of the Rhodesia Native Regiment arrived in East Africa, everything they needed had to be carried in by humans, a huge army of porters.

Koos was not generally given to feeling much compassion for blacks, but he could not avoid pity for these men – clad in rags, barefoot, completely exposed to the elements, and expected to carry heavy packs of rations or ammunition for miles every day over the same appalling ground that he had to traverse. Inadequate as his food often was, he suspected that the African porters fared even worse. It was hardly surprising that so many of them simply succumbed to exhaustion, often just dropping out on the march, to be left by the roadside to recover, if they were lucky or, more likely, to supplement the diet of the hyenas and other carnivorous scavengers that infested the bush about them.

The German schutztruppe did not have quite the same problem as far as rations were concerned. They tended to live off the land and were evidently ruthless in expropriating from the local natives whatever they wanted. This meant that by the time Koos and his fellows arrived in an area, their chances of finding food there, even if they were willing to pay for it, were very small. Koos could not remember when he had last had a really satisfying meal. Often the daily fare was half a tin of bully beef and a couple of very dry biscuits and on many occasions he had been obliged to share the rations of the black soldiers – ugali, a sort of corn-meal porridge. Sometimes the officers were able to shoot some game to supplement the diet of themselves and their soldiers, though this was seldom practicable, and for one glorious month they had attached to the unit a small herd of rather scrawny cattle, which had temporarily raised the standard of provisions. In general, though, there were, as they joked, two levels of rations – 'not enough', and 'not nearly enough'.

These harsh conditions would have been easier to bear had you been in good health, but it was fair to say that virtually nobody in this army, from the staff officers downwards, was in good health. Dysentery was a fact of life, seldom severe enough to put you out of action, but usually enough to sap your energy and enthusiasm. Malaria was endemic, and despite the use of quinine, affected almost everybody at some time. Koos himself had suffered two bouts, the first severe enough to confine him to a rough cot in the field hospital for a few days, and it was very seldom that every soldier in his platoon was fit for duty. Perhaps the most insidious and unpleasant affliction was caused by a tiny creature called a jigger. This little flea would burrow into the skin of your foot and lay its eggs in a sac there, often beneath a toenail. Given that virtually none of the African soldiers or porters wore boots or even sandals, the jigger's opportunities for colonization were considerable. The sac had to be removed, painfully, preferably with the aid of a sterilized needle (often not available in the field), and the chances of infection were high. Even at the field hospitals it was difficult, often impossible, to maintain proper standards of hygiene, and quite minor wounds could have serious consequences. Koos remembered only too well a young English lad serving with a South African unit next to theirs who had cut his hand clearing the bush for a camp. The wound had become infected, septicaemia had set in, and within three days the boy was dead. He lay now beneath a wooden cross in the lonely bush, thousands of miles from home.

Koos' melancholy reflections were interrupted by the arrival of his superior officer who emerged from the darkness and scrambled down into the rough trench that they had dug when they arrived here two days before.

"Koos, I've just been talking to the captain." Second Lieutenant Humphrey Nayland's face, lean and serious, was pale in the moonlight, and he spoke in a low voice. "He wants us to take out a small patrol to see if we can find out what the Hun is up to."

When they had moved in to the village of Malangali they had received reports from the inhabitants that there was a substantial German force in the vicinity, but there had so far been no sign of them.

"How many men do we need, Humphrey?"

"I was thinking maybe four, apart from you and me – Mpika, Ndlovu and a couple of the other more reliable chaps."

"Very good. I'll round them up."

Koos moved quietly along to the next dug-out and got the sentry to rouse the men he wanted. Before long they had joined him. Most of the men in the unit were of the Shona tribe – the recruitment officers attempted, for obvious reasons, to allocate to each unit within the regiment men who spoke the same language. Koos himself was fluent in Shona and he admired Humphrey for the way he had, within quite a short time, been able to acquire a good working knowledge of the tongue.

Innocent Mpika was an exception to the ethnic uniformity of the unit. A native of Northern Rhodesia, he had been working in a mine near Que Que in Southern Rhodesia when the word went out about the formation of a black Rhodesian regiment. Innocent had joined up straight away. Educated on a mission in the north of his country, where the fathers had bestowed upon him his somewhat challenging name, he spoke reasonably good English and was also competent in Shona, which had some similarities to his own native tongue. He even had a smattering of Afrikaans, acquired from the supervisors at the mine. In the months they had served together, both Koos and Humphrey had developed a great deal of respect for Innocent, who had shown himself to be resourceful and reliable, with a considerable capacity for courage and coolness under fire. He also had a good sense of humour. Koos was checking the sentries one evening and had asked Innocent if he had seen any German askaris. He replied that he had not, and then added, straight-faced, "but it is night, and they are black!"

The six men crowded into Koos' dugout for the briefing.

"Tell them we're just after information – looking for any sign of the Germans," explained Humphrey. "No shooting if we can avoid it. We'll make our way up to the top of the ridge to the west. The sun will be up by then, so we should be able to see down into the valley beyond and tell if there is any activity there."

Koos quietly explained the plan to the four troopers who nodded silently.

"You go first, Ndlovu, then the Lieutenant. Mpika and I will walk at the back." Ndlovu had worked some years before for the legendary hunter, Frederick Selous, and had acquired an extraordinary ability to move silently through the bush and read the unwritten signs of the jungle.

Koos summoned one of the other African troopers to occupy his dugout, and the six men then moved out, walking slowly in single file, rifles at the ready. Koos kept his eyes fixed on the back of Private Zamani, walking in front of him, and listened for any sound other than the quiet rustling of his companions making their way along the game trail towards the ridge. Every minute or so they would stop and strain their eyes and ears for any evidence that they were not alone. Not a sound. The moon had long gone down, but the stars were bright, and after a while a very faint glow on the western horizon gave a hint of the approach of dawn. Once a night-jar erupted from the path in front with a frantic flurry of wings, and Koos froze, his heart thumping.

As the dawn light got stronger and his eyes became accustomed to the dark, Koos could make out the shadowy shapes of the trees overhanging the path and could even sometimes see the backs of Humphrey and Ndlovu, ten paces in front. They walked for about an hour, the last part up a steep slope as they climbed up the ridge. All of a sudden, Zamani stopped. Peering ahead through the gloom. Koos could see that the whole patrol had come to a halt. They were about to enter a large clearing which Koos guessed must be near the top of the ridge. Humphrey and Ndlovu had their heads together and were presumably deciding whether to follow the track across the clearing or instead remain in cover and go around it. He glanced behind him. Mpika was not in sight. When he looked forward again he could see that the decision had been taken and the patrol was on the move across the clearing.

He was probably five paces into the open when suddenly the peace of the early morning was horribly shattered. From both sides of the clearing the air was split with rifle flashes and what seemed a deafening sound of fire. He heard a thump and a strange cough from the man in front as he threw himself down on the ground and lay there, pulse racing, throat dry and sweaty hands grasping the rifle beneath him.

For what seemed an eternity he lay there, though it was probably less than half a minute. Then he lifted his head slowly out of the dirt. Nothing. He could see nothing. The grass they were in was long enough to conceal them from the enemy but also prevented them from doing anything but lie there.

"Humphrey!" he called out in a low voice, "are you alright?"

"Yes – I'm fine," came the reply. "They missed me but I think Ndlovu has been hit."

Then a voice came from the jungle over to Koos' left, speaking in heavily accented English.

"English soldiers, we are surround you. No use fight. Stand up, leave weapons on ground. We will not shoot."

There was a pause, then Koos heard Humphrey say "Alright! We'll do as you say! Stand up, men!"

Koos got to his feet. In front of him he could see Humphrey rising and behind him Private Mpango. There was no sign of movement from Ndlovu or Zamani and he could hear nothing behind him. He did not dare to turn around.

The voice sounded again, more urgently. "All stand! All! Keep hands above! Nobody stay down. We shoot!"

Humphrey responded at once. "Don't shoot! The others cannot stand. They are wounded, already shot. They cannot harm you!"

There was a long pause during which presumably the German soldier digested this information and perhaps consulted his colleagues. Then he spoke again.

"So! You stay standing until we come. No do anything. Keep hands above. No move, or we shoot. This time we not miss."

After a short time, Koos could see two askaris approaching from his left and another four from his right. All had their rifles at the ready, pointing in his direction. One of the askaris stopped a few feet away while his fellow came round behind Koos and pushed him roughly to the side off the path. Koos stumbled and nearly fell. As he recovered his balance he could see the man who had pushed him pick up his rifle and then cautiously go forward to look at Zamani, who had not moved. The German askari turned Zamani's body over and peered closely at it. He said something to his colleague in a language Koos did not understand, and picked up Zamani's rifle. The other askari then moved behind Koos and prodded him roughly with his rifle so that he had to go forward. Ahead he could see Humphrey and Mpango, both also with rifles in their backs. Ndlovu lay at their feet. He was moaning quietly.

He heard Humphrey say, "You can't leave him there! He's wounded. He needs a doctor." The askaris ignored him and pushed him and Mpango forward down the path. Humphrey raised his voice and turned his head towards the bushes whence the commands had come.

"We have a badly wounded man. He needs medical attention. For pity's sake!"

"Simama!" The voice rang out and the askaris stopped. From the jungle into the clearing stepped a man. As he approached, Koos could see that he was quite short and muscular. He was very black but his curly hair was grizzled. Unlike the other askaris, he wore nothing on his head and was not carrying a rifle. He had what appeared to be a pistol in a holster tied around his waist. Koos could see no insignia on his clothing, but he was clearly the man in charge. He was quiet and confident and his gaze was unflinching. He reminded Koos, in a strange way, of a bull terrier his parents still had at the farm. He glanced sharply up at the three British soldiers standing before him with their arms in the air and then looked down at the wounded man. He paused in thought for a moment and then made up his mind.

"So! We take him! You!" he pointed to Koos and Mpango, "you carry! No far! We go!"

Koos and Mpango bent down and lifted Ndlovu up by each arm. He cried out in agony as they took his weight but then mercifully passed out. Koos caught Humphrey's eye and saw him mouth the name "Mpika?" but shook his head imperceptibly. He had no idea.

Slowly they made their way up the track as the morning sun began to bring the bush to life.

§

As the man had said, it was not far, and in ten minutes or so the group, which consisted of about fifteen German askaris, arrived at the main camp, spread out among the trees on the western side of the ridge that had been the patrol's target. As Koos looked around he could see men emerging from their bivouacs and sitting around eating their breakfast. Some residual smoke still trickled up from the fires used for cooking which had presumably been extinguished so that no tell-tale plumes would be visible to hostile observers. At their captors' instruction, they had laid Ndlovu, who had regained consciousness and was groaning in pain, on the ground next to two other recumbent figures. A tall, thin African, presumably the medical orderly, had examined him and produced bandages to cover his wounds. He appeared to have been shot twice, once in the thigh and again in the side, but clearly neither bullet had struck a major blood vessel or no doubt he would by now have bled to death.

Bull terrier gestured to Humphrey and Koos to follow him and led them across the camp site. Their escorting askaris followed, rifles still at the ready. Seated on a bank beneath the trees, Koos saw three white soldiers eating. Their captor went up to the one in the middle of the group and saluted him. He spoke briefly to him, presumably in Kiswahili, which Koos knew was the lingua franca of the region, generally used by the German troops and, indeed, by many of the British units. The German, evidently the officer in charge, seemed annoyed and there was what seemed to be a somewhat acerbic exchange of views. Eventually the officer shrugged, got to his feet and came over to them. He was a lean muscular man, of about medium height, with a beaky nose above a bushy full beard. He stared hard at the two British soldiers.

"Who are you?" he demanded in English.

"I am Lieutenant Nayland," replied Humphrey, "and this is Sergeant van Rensburg."

The officer glanced sharply at Koos.

"Van Rensburg? Are you an Afrikaner?" The question was asked in faultless Afrikaans.

"Well … yes!" Koos was amazed. Clearly this man was not German at all.

"So! Why are you fighting for the damned English? You are a traitor!"

"No, I am not!" retorted Koos indignantly. "South Africa is part of the British Empire now. We are fighting together against the

Germans. Smuts and Botha are leading us!"

"Ja, well they are traitors too!" The officer spoke with deep contempt. "Where have you come from?"

Koos glanced across at Humphrey.

"What does he want, Koos?"

"He wants to know where we are from. He is not German. He is a Dutchman."

Humphrey faced the officer. "We have told you everything we can. We are just the scouts for a very powerful force. You would do well to retreat while you can."

The German officer laughed sarcastically. "Ja! Ja! We shall see. I think your comrades have heard the shots and, when you do not return, they will know what has happened to you. But it does not matter now. Soon they will be dead or prisoners like you."

He turned to the bull terrier and gave him some terse instructions in Kiswahili. The man nodded his head and in turn spoke to the two askaris guarding Koos and Humphrey who turned them roughly around and pushed them back the way they had come to the place where Ndlovu was lying. When they got there bull terrier motioned to them to sit.

"You stay!" he said. "You sit! Not run or …" He made a shooting gesture.

As Koos and Humphrey sat there, they could see that the soldiers were getting ready to move and within quite a short time were formed up in a body. Evidently the only ones to be left behind would be the sick and wounded men, the medical orderly, Koos, Humphrey, Mpango and two guards.

One of the other German officers came over and looked down at them.

"So, gentlemen, have a peaceful morning!"

"You speak good English," said Humphrey.

"Ja," said the German, "I spent a year working in a shipping office in Mombasa. It has been useful when we have had English prisoners". He smiled down at them.

"Let me give you some advice, Englishmen. Do not try to

escape. These men will shoot you down without hesitation. Kapitan Vermeulen would be happy for that to happen. He hates the English."

"What did you say his name was?" asked Humphrey.

"Vermeulen – Oskar Vermeulen." The German looked at Koos and smiled. "He is a Dutchman like you, but he is a good soldier and loyal to the German Empire." He glanced over his shoulder to where the German askaris were moving off over the ridge.

"So, Englishmen, auf wiedersehn. Remember what I said." And he went.

When he had passed out of earshot, Koos said to Humphrey "Does the captain's name mean anything to you?"

"Maybe. Do you remember, Koos, that Dutch lady that I told you about, who was so kind to me in Bloemfontein?"

"Ja, I remember you telling me of her."

"Well her name was Vermeulen, and she had a husband whom she hadn't seen for many years. I am sure his name was Oskar. She told me she had heard that he had gone farming in German East Africa."

"And you think this is him?"

"Yes I do. She had a son whom I met, and he very much has the look of this man."

Koos thought about this for a few moments.

"Maybe we don't tell the kapitan about this?"

Humphrey laughed shortly. "I think we definitely don't tell him about this!"

§

They stayed under the trees as the sun rose and the heat increased. The medical orderly brought them cold ugali and some rather tepid and nasty-tasting water. Ndlovu was still evidently in a good deal of pain, but was able to sit up and drink. About an hour after the German force had left, they could hear distant sounds of musketry which went on for a long time. There was also a rumbling boom. Koos glanced across at Humphrey. They both knew that the British force at Malangali had no artillery. Any guns in action had to be German, which did not bode well for the defenders.

After a while, one of the guarding askaris stood up to stretch his legs. He was careful to keep both his eyes and his rifle trained on his captives. Suddenly he was hurled forward and immediately afterwards Koos heard the crack of a rifle shot. The other askari whirled round in the direction of the shooting but there was a second shot which sent him sprawling too. It had all happened in a matter of seconds, and the three captives and the medical orderly were frozen with shock before they too flung themselves to the dirt.

Koos raised his head and saw a figure emerging from the bushes some 30 yards away, advancing slowly with rifle at the ready. Innocent Mpika!

CHAPTER ELEVEN

INNOCENT

As the last man in the patrol, Innocent had walked carefully along some five yards behind his sergeant, his rifle at the ready and his ears and eyes straining for signs of trouble from the bush around them. When they paused at the clearing, he suddenly got a very strong feeling that they were in great danger. He did not immediately follow Koos but hung back in the bush and was still standing there when the shocking fusillade shattered the dawn calm. Like his fellows, he flung himself flat on the ground and lay there, heart thumping uncontrollably, his mouth dry, and his body cringing from the prospect of a further murderous assault. Lying there, face down in the grass with his rifle clutched in both hands in front of him, he heard the exchange of commands and pleas between his comrades and the enemy. As the minutes went by, he realized that the Germans did not know he was there. He continued to lie, hardly breathing, not daring to raise his head.

After what seemed an age, he heard the others all moving away up the path. He forced himself to remain still for a minute and another minute. Then he cautiously raised his head and listened. Silence. Slowly he got to his feet and let circulation back into his cramped limbs. The dawn light was quite strong now and looking across the clearing, Innocent could see a bundle lying in the grass just off the track about half-way across. He moved slowly up to it and discovered the body of the hapless Zamani. He was quite dead, half his face shot away and blood soaking his tunic.

Innocent retreated once more to the relative safety of the bush and squatted down while he considered his options. The obvious thing to do was to return to base and report what had happened. There was very little likelihood of encountering more enemy troops between where he was and the British camp at Malangali. The most dangerous part of the journey would probably be gaining the safety of his unit's lines without getting shot by a sentry. On the other hand, to do this would mean abandoning his comrades for whom, after sharing a life of danger and hardship for many months, he had a great deal of respect and affection. This applied especially to Corporal Ndlovu, who had become a good friend, and also, in a strange way, to his commanding officer. Lieutenant Nayland had shown himself to be a decent and sensible young man, commendably free of the arrogance and sense of superiority that imbued so many of his race. He had always treated Innocent with respect, just like a fellow human being, not an attitude that Innocent had commonly encountered among the Europeans of his acquaintance. To abandon his friends to a fate unknown went against the grain. Moreover, they had not obtained the information they were sent out to get. Beyond the fact that there was a German force in the vicinity with sufficient numbers and fire-power to wipe out a small patrol, they knew nothing.

Innocent had many admirable qualities, and among them were loyalty and a deep-seated stubbornness. The first of these had, paradoxically, been the cause of his initial exile. Two years of severe drought had brought his village to the brink of starvation and the only way he saw of providing for the family he loved had been to travel south and find paid employment at a mine in Southern Rhodesia. Leaving had been hard: it had now been over two years since he had seen his beloved Lillian, and his two little sons, now six and eight years old, would very likely not recognize him. However, he knew it was what had to be done and he had stuck to it. His decision to enlist in the Regiment had been motivated not a little by the belief that it might take him home, since it was rumoured that they would be operating in the eastern province of his land, but this had turned out to be a false hope. After training in Southern Rhodesia, they had transferred immediately to the war zone in German East Africa.

These two qualities guided his decision now, to try find out the fate of his friends and, in so doing, to get the military information that they had been tasked to discover. The question was just how best to put this plan into effect. From what he had heard, the main German force was probably quite close – "no far" the German askari had said. Following along the same path would be unwise. The likelihood of a second ambush was remote, but it was certain that there would be sentries on duty who would see him. The answer seemed to be to make a wide loop through the bush and approach the German camp from the side or even from the back. The clearing was near the crest of the ridge, and Innocent reasoned that, if the camp really was quite close, it was very likely just on the other side of the hill. The trick was going to be to get into a position to overlook it without being seen or heard by the defenders.

The disadvantage of the flanking move was that it obliged him to abandon the path and move through the uncleared bush which was inevitably slow and laborious, especially as he had to try to make as little noise as possible. Fortunately, after a couple of hundred yards of painfully slow progress, he happened on another game trail. Although this was taking him diagonally away from his intended objective, the greater speed and ease of movement justified the diversion. After he had crossed the ridge and descended a short way on the other side, he struck back through the thicket towards where he expected the camp to be.

Once again, progress was snail-like, and it was probably nearly three hours after he had left the clearing that he unexpectedly stepped clear of a bush he had been wriggling through and found himself looking down on what was clearly a camp site. As soon as he saw it he dropped down on all fours and drew back into the bush from which he had just emerged, and lay there, his heart racing and his ears straining for voices and other sounds that might tell him he had been seen. Hearing nothing to suggest alarm, he peered cautiously through the leaves of the bush that concealed him.

Before him lay an open area that had accommodated a number of men, though there was no sign of life now. There were several rough bivouacs scattered among the trees, and one slightly more elaborate one with a groundsheet suspended from the branches over two camp beds. He could see the remains of a number of small fires. As he watched, his eye was caught by a movement to the left of the scene and he froze. A black man in the uniform of the German schutztruppe came into view. He was carrying a rifle held at the ready. Innocent remained motionless until the man turned and disappeared again from sight, and then he slowly worked his way further round to the right so he could get a better view of the part of the camp site that the soldier had come from. When he parted the leaves again and looked through he felt a surge of elation. Sitting on a log little more than a stone's throw away were the Lieutenant and Sergeant van Rensburg and he recognized Mpango seated not far away. There were several others lying on the ground but he could not see who they were. There appeared to be three German askaris. As far as he could see, only two of them were armed. He could now, he thought, see the whole of the camp site and there appeared to be no-one else there. These men were its sole occupants.

Innocent watched for a minute or two while he decided what to do. He was fairly confident that he could bring down the German soldiers, at least the two armed ones, but it would require very swift and accurate shooting. The odds would be improved, though, if he could get a little closer. Looking along the clearing to his left, he saw that if he could move a hundred yards or so in that direction, he could get quite a bit nearer without being seen. So, moving with painstaking care to avoid making the slightest noise, he set off. After crawling slowly along for what seemed an age but was probably only fifteen or twenty minutes, he reckoned he should have gone far enough. When he inched forward and peered cautiously through the leaves he saw that he had judged it to perfection. His three comrades were sitting, heads down, facing in his direction. Two of the German askaris were seated with their backs to him. The third German soldier, the one who did not seem to be armed, was bending over one of the recumbent bodies. The nearest man was hardly 30 yards away.

Innocent breathed in deeply and tried to will his heart-rate to slow down. He would only get one chance. He raised himself onto one knee and lifted his rifle slowly up to aim. He waited until the sight was squarely in the middle of his target's back before releasing the safety-catch – it was not unknown with this weapon for the release of the safety-catch to trigger a discharge. As he did so, the askari he was aiming at stood up and moved to his right, still facing away from him. Innocent held his breath and followed the man with his rifle until he stopped after a few paces. Then he lined up again, breathed out, and squeezed the trigger.

The shocking crash of the shot was still ringing in his ears as he worked the bolt as quickly as he could and moved the sight back to the other soldier. This man committed what was probably a tactical blunder in springing to his feet and whirling around to bring his own weapon to face the assault. He was much too late. Innocent's second bullet, released two seconds after the first, struck him in the middle of the chest and hurled him backwards. The fight was over in moments.

§

The greetings were brief but heartfelt. Humphrey gripped Innocent warmly by the hand.

"Well done, Mpika! Jolly good show! You've saved our bacon!"

They checked the two shot schutztruppe. The first was quite dead. The second was alive, his eyes staring wide with shock and blood trickling from his mouth. They relieved him and his companion of their rifles and what ammunition they were carrying. Of their own weapons there was no sign. The main German force must have taken them.

"We must get out of here" said the Lieutenant. "They will be back. You will have to guide us, Mpika."

"Yes, effendi. What will we do with him?" They all looked down at Ndlovu, lying there grey-faced and sweating, obviously in a good deal of pain.

"He must stay here," said the sergeant firmly. "We cannot carry him. It is impossible, man."

Ndlovu looked pleadingly up at Innocent.

"Do not leave me!" he said in Shona."They will kill me or let me be eaten by the hyenas!"

"We must not leave him here," said Innocent in English to be sure that his officer would understand. "They will not be careful for him."

He watched while Humphrey looked around and assessed the situation. Finally, he evidently made up his mind, and turned to the medical orderly who had been sitting on the ground, frightened and apprehensive.

"You have a stretcher?" He gestured with a carrying motion. It took a little while before he was understood, but then the orderly revealed that one of the two sick German askaris under his care was lying on a rough stretcher. They lifted the man off and laid him back on the ground. The stretcher was a home-made affair, fashioned from two poles with a blanket doubled over stretched between them. Innocent and Mpango lifted Ndlovu up onto the stretcher. The wounded man grimaced with pain but he whispered "thank you" as they laid him down.

"You and Mpango carry him," said Humphrey to Innocent."I will lead and Sergeant van Rensburg will guard the rear. You!" he motioned to the orderly "you stay here!" The orderly nodded eagerly, only too anxious to comply.

They filled their water-bottles from the German storage barrel and then set out, Humphrey in front with Innocent's rifle, followed by the stretcher-bearers, and Koos at the back carrying the German Mausers.

§

With silence no longer being important, they were able to retrace Innocent's path much more quickly. It was still very hard work, though, and by the time they regained the game trail, Innocent was glad of the chance to lay his burden on the ground and relieve his aching limbs. They all had a drink of water and the sergeant produced a handful of biltong from the pocket of his bush jacket which he shared with the lieutenant and then, after only a moment's hesitation, with the other men. Innocent chewed his biltong with relish. The salty dried meat, a last relic of the halcyon days of their unit cattle herd, was delicious. He realized he had eaten nothing since a portion of cold ugali hurriedly consumed before they set out in the early morning, and he was extremely hungry.

"Do you know where this trail leads?" asked Humphrey.

"No, effendi," replied Innocent. "I joined it near the place where we were attacked. But I think it goes in the direction of our camp."

"Right!" said Humphrey. "Then we will follow it and see what happens." He looked sympathetically at Innocent. "Tell me when you need to rest and we will stop."

Innocent and Mpango picked up the stretcher and they all made their way up towards the top of the ridge. Although progress was a lot easier down the game trail, it was still hard work, especially for the two men carrying the unfortunate Ndlovu. While, as Innocent wryly reflected, it was a good thing that the normal users of the trail were evidently not of immense stature, so that the likelihood of the unwelcome appearance of a buffalo or a rhino was very small, it did also mean that it was often necessary to crouch low down to get through, hard enough for unencumbered humans but much more difficult for stretcher-bearers. The lieutenant did what he could to clear the bushes with the butt of his rifle, but they all regretted the absence of that invaluable local machete, the panga.

Once they had crossed the ridge, they could hear the distant sound of spasmodic rifle-fire, interspersed with the occasional boom of the gun that they had heard before. The trail seemed to follow a roughly parallel course to the path they had originally taken that morning. At one point they crossed a small stream and were able to fill their bottles with clear, cold water. The sound of gunfire grew ever louder and eventually, when they reached a small clearing, Humphrey gestured to them to stop. They laid Ndlovu gently down on a bank of ferns in the shade. He lay with his eyes closed, his face a mask of pain. For the last hour or so he had lain silent, only occasionally emitting a groan when his carriers unwittingly jarred the stretcher or it came in contact with a branch as they were lifting him through. The field-dressings that had been applied to his wounds back in the German camp were soaked with his blood. Innocent looked at his friend with worried eyes. If he did not get proper medical attention soon, he would not survive.

The lieutenant spoke quietly.

"We must be getting very near the German line. I think they have probably surrounded our fellows and if we just keep going we are going to run into them."

They were all well aware that their force in Malangali was not large – no more than a company. The German unit that they had seen was of similar size, and there was no doubt there were more enemy troops, given the audible presence of at least one artillery piece which the unit they had seen did not have.

"If we all go on," said the lieutenant, "it is going to be difficult. We are sure to be seen. Sergeant van Rensburg, I want you to stay here with Mpango and Corporal Ndlovu. Keep hidden and wait. Mpika and I will try and get through to our lines and then we'll get reinforcements and come for you. We'll leave you the two German guns."

"What if you don't come back?" asked the sergeant.

"Then you will have to decide what is best. If all else fails, you might have to surrender again to the enemy." The lieutenant smiled wryly. "If that happens, you might want to chuck the rifles away into the bush. The enemy may not be happy with you if they find you with two of their weapons!"

§

Innocent followed his superior officer as they made their way cautiously on down the trail. He had resumed possession of his rifle and Humphrey was clearing a way for them through the overhanging branches with his hands. They had not heard any sustained sounds of gunfire for a while, just the occasional rifle shot suggesting that the battle was not yet over. Knowing that they must be getting near the enemy positions, they once more did their best to move as silently as possible. It was now late afternoon, and Innocent knew that the short tropical evening would soon come and go, leaving them in complete darkness until the moon rose later. Progress would then become very difficult. Every minute or so, they stopped and listened in silence for any human sounds. Innocent straightened up behind Humphrey as the trail emerged into a small glade in the forest and then they both stopped abruptly. Crossing the glade diagonally in front of them was a much more substantial track, looking like a human thoroughfare. Before they had time to take this in a man emerged from the bush on the track from their right. He was an African clad in a shirt and loincloth and he carried an axe over his shoulder and a panga in his right hand. He saw them immediately and half-turned to flee but then must have seen their uniforms and turned back.

"Waingereza?" he asked.

"Ndio, yes," said Innocent and Humphrey together eagerly. English!

Humphrey pointed at the path behind the man.

"Malangali?" The man nodded.

"Will you take us?" Humphrey gestured to show what he meant. The man thought about this for a moment and then nodded. He summoned them to him with his hand and raised a finger to his lips to indicate silence. He then turned and went back the way he had come, this time with the two soldiers on his heels. Innocent clasped his rifle at the ready in case of trouble.

They had followed the track for no more than a quarter of a mile when it led over a rough wooden bridge across a small stream, probably the same one they had filled their water bottles from earlier in the afternoon. Before they crossed it, though, their guide went off the track and into the water. They walked down the stream, which passed through a cleft in the hill. Soon after they emerged from this, the man scrambled out of the stream and took them along a rough but fairly well-used path up the slope. As they neared the top they were brought to an abrupt stop.

"Halt! Who goes there?" Thankfully in English!

Their guide went forward. He had presumably passed the same sentry on his way out not long before and he gestured behind him to where Humphrey and Innocent were waiting.

There was a joyful exclamation and "Welcome back!" in Shona. They had made it!

§

They were taken to the company commander, Captain Longwood, who shook both men warmly by the hand.

"We thought you were gone, for sure!" he said to Humphrey.

"Well, we would have been, but for Mpika here," replied the lieutenant. "He was an absolute hero! We owe him our lives."

Innocent felt a warm flush of embarrassment.

"No, effendi! I was only doing my duty."

'Maybe," said Humphrey, "but not everyone does it that well. I will not forget! But we have three other men out there, sir, one of them badly wounded. We must go back and bring them in."

"Well you're not going now," said the captain firmly. "I cannot risk any men at the moment. We are surrounded and they obviously have a good many more men than we do. We have beaten off several attacks today, but they'll try again. As you can see," he indicated a nearby shell crater and a couple of destroyed huts in the village, "they have a gun, although I suspect they may be a bit short of ammo – we only get shelled when they are about to attack. In any case, it will be dark in a couple of minutes. We'll see what we may be able to do in the morning."

"Are there any reinforcements on the way?" asked Humphrey.

"I just don't know. We were told that Colonel Murray and his Rhodesians were in the area, but we haven't seen hide nor hair of them yet. We're just going to have to do the best we can."

Innocent returned to the dug-out he had left what seemed an age ago, although it was in fact merely 12 hours before. His comrades were delighted to welcome him back, though naturally very sorry to hear the bad news of Zamani's death and Ndlovu's injuries. His platoon had survived the day's battle with only two minor wounds, although there had been three men killed elsewhere in the company, and several others badly hurt. With the threat of a further assault from the German side, half of all the soldiers had to stand to, with the remainder trying to catch a few hours sleep curled up in the dugout. Despite his weariness, Innocent found it very difficult to sleep, and the next dawn found him hardly rested at all.

With the rising sun, everybody was back on guard, ready for the attack they knew must come. It was no surprise, just as the sun started to bring a glow to the eastern sky, when there was a sudden tremendous outburst of gunfire, rifles and machine guns, from one section of the German lines. None of the fire, however, appeared to be directed at them, nor was there any sign of enemy soldiers charging over the ground towards them. The captain shouted to all to hold their fire and wait until they saw a target. Suddenly one of his companions shouted "Look!" and pointed towards the German line. In the dim dawn light, Innocent could see, a few hundred yards away, indistinct figures leaving their positions and moving away to the east, towards the sound of gunfire. Clearly there was a different battle going on! They heard the artillery piece fire twice, neither round falling anywhere near the village, and then it fell silent.

The sounds of conflict continued with great intensity for nearly half an hour, and then gradually faded to spasmodic rifle-fire. Suddenly, from the direction of the battle noises, they saw a small group of men running over the open ground towards them. The captain ordered "Wait for my command!" and then "Hold your fire! Hold your fire! They're friends!" As they got closer, Innocent could see that they were white soldiers, wearing the distinctive khaki topis of the British troops in East Africa. The Rhodesians had arrived!

CORRESPONDENCE – 5

Mrs Louisa Nayland
The Vicarage
Cowdenhall
Yorkshire

January 1917

Dearest Mother

It was so wonderful to get all your letters and Molly's when we arrived here a day or two ago. I am not allowed to tell you where we are but it is quite a decent little place, the food is a good deal better than we have been used to, we are sleeping in proper tents and, best of all – the mail!

They are giving us a few days to rest and regroup before we move on. Every time we think we've got Von Lettow-Vorbeck, the German commander, cornered, he manages to slip away, but we'll catch up with the rascal soon!

We had a bit of excitement the other day when a patrol I was leading was captured by the enemy. We might still be prisoners if not for the heroic efforts of one of my African troopers who showed tremendous pluck and initiative in rescuing us. I've recommended him for a DCM and I hope he gets it. He certainly deserves to! He's been promoted to corporal anyway. His name – you'll love this, mother – is Innocent! I think his parents were influenced by some Roman Catholic missionaries working in the place where he was born. Weren't there several Popes called Innocent? It is rather a strange name for a soldier, but then of course they wouldn't have known he was going to turn out as one. He is a fine fellow, and speaks quite decent English for an African.

Koos is well, as am I. We ran into a unit of the old BSAP recently and guess who was in charge? Marcus! He seemed well, apart from the fever which we all get from time to time – I think it's a part of living in Africa. He particularly asked to be remembered to you and Father.

I sorted all your letters and Molly's into date order before I read them. I can't tell you how much I enjoyed that - getting all your news. Dear old England seems such a long way away. It's another life. BUT why do you not say anything at all about Ruth? Molly speaks of having met her a couple of times and that she's living in York now, but doesn't really explain why. Are Albert Moffat and Emily still living in the village or have they moved too? After those first few letters I got from her when I was first in South Africa, I haven't had any and she has not replied to any of mine. I sent several direct to the farm and a couple care of Molly for her to pass on, but nothing! I don't understand it!

Oh, by the way, I've just been promoted – Acting Lieutenant Nayland! Doesn't mean much, really, except I could have a second pip on my shoulders if we bothered with that sort of thing out here (we don't!).

I'm enclosing a letter to Moll with yours and I do hope they both get there and you don't have to wait too long. Please don't worry if you don't hear from me for long periods. It's really impossible to write when we're out in the bush so it's only when I get back to civilization (relatively speaking!) that I can sit down and put pen to paper. I'd say we'll be off back into the bush in a couple of days, so it may be a while before you hear from me again.

Do give my love to Father and any of the others you may be seeing (I suppose Oliver and Moll are still in France and Gertie in Canada?). Give Dizzy a special pat from me. I was very glad to know that he is still going strong, though sorry to hear the sad story about the chicken. Father must have been very annoyed! I bet Dizzy wasn't remorseful, though!

PLEASE let me know about Ruth.

With much love

Humphrey

On active service
Somewhere in East Africa!

CHAPTER TWELVE

OLIVER

Oliver had been to France twice before the war. The most recent visit had been quite a brief one in 1913 when he was part of a British military mission inspecting the French forts around Verdun. Apart from touring the very impressive, but he now realized from bitter experience, mostly ineffective, fortifications, much of their time seemed to have been spent in a succession of French army messes imbibing an astonishing quantity of truly excellent wine. The champagne had led into the burgundy, the burgundy to the claret, and the evenings were generally finished off with a glass, or several, of cognac. The experience had left Oliver with a keen appreciation of the stock in trade of the Gallic vignerons. However, it would have given him little appreciation and understanding of the country and its people, apart from its young army officers.

Fortunately this soldierly foray had not been his only French experience. In the summer after he had finished school, he and two of his classmates had spent several weeks rambling around the country. Inspired by youthful curiosity and enthusiasm, assisted by a smattering of schoolroom French, and guided by one of Herr Baedeker's excellent publications, they had started in Normandy then made their way up the Loire Valley towards Paris. A week in that exciting city had been an amazing experience for three quite strait-laced English schoolboys. It had also somewhat depleted their resources so, not without regret, they had travelled north again, through Soissons, St Quentin and Arras, before catching a train to Calais to board the ferry-boat back to Dover.

Oliver could still remember the images of that late shining time – the golden acres of the ripening crops, the rolling pastures kept green by the summer rain, the deeper green of the woods that filled the valleys. In the little towns and villages that nestled comfortably into the countryside, they had stayed in an auberge if there was one, or sometimes lodged with a local farmer or householder. In the evening they would sit with a carafe of vin ordinaire outside a small estaminet and watch the life of the village go on – women bringing in the washing from where it had been hanging on the balconies, children scampering around and shouting to each other, perhaps a farmer returning from delivering produce, driving his cart slowly over the cobbles between the rough stone buildings. The old men of the village would usually also be sitting on the benches of the estaminet, viewing the rest of life through rheumy, cynical eyes. Despite the language barrier (an understanding that "Avez vous vue la plume de ma tante?" means "Have you seen my aunt's pen?" was of limited value in exchanging pleasantries in a rural café) there would often be an exchange of nods and smiles between the two parties, and not infrequently a round of toasts – La Reine! (Queen Victoria), La Republique! La Liberte! Some of the old men had evidently served in the disastrous Franco-Prussian war 30 years before, and they would raise their glasses with a bitter sneer and growl "A bas les Boches!", a sentiment that Oliver and his fellows were happy to echo.

As Oliver and his men walked now towards their forward position, up the road pot-holed and rutted, lined with the debris of war – smashed and abandoned carts, broken cases, the bloated corpses of mules and horses – it was difficult to believe that this could be the same landscape. The fields were brown and pitted with shell craters, the woods mostly reduced to splintered stumps poking up through the mire. The neat and homely little settlements had been reduced to rubble, their human inhabitants driven back further behind the battle lines where a semblance of normality could still be found. They had just passed through the town of Albert, famous for its gilded statue of the Madonna and Child standing atop the steeple of the church in the middle of town. Now gunfire had all but destroyed the church, and the Madonna hung grotesquely leaning sideways from the remains of the spire over the square. Oliver remembered hearing that it was said that when the Madonna finally fell, the war would end!

As they neared the start of the communication trenches that would take them up to the front line, they could hear the occasional boom of the artillery and spasmodic crackling of small arms fire. From time to time a shell would whistle overhead to explode somewhere to their rear. The soldiers, nearly all veterans of many months' service, plodded on without reacting. Soon they reached the start of the trenches and Oliver told Sergeant-Major Brasher to fall the men out by the road-side for a few minutes. Most took the opportunity for a drink and a biscuit.

"Now then, lads," said Brasher, "last free pee!" There was some sarcastic laughter, but a number of men took up the offer.

"Right, men," said Oliver after a few minutes. "Time to go. Keep your heads down!"

As they made their way along the communication trench, the sounds of battle grew louder and bullets could be heard fizzing overhead and occasionally smacking into to the nearby earth with a dull splat. Before too long they were in the front line trench and taking over the positions from the unit they were relieving. Oliver spoke briefly to the company commander, a young captain in the Royal Fusiliers, his face grey with fatigue.

"Been pretty quiet the last forty-eight hours," he said. "I'm sure that'll change now that you chaps are here." He gave a brief humourless laugh and shook Oliver's hand. "Good luck!"

And then he was gone.

Oliver went round his section of the trench, checking that his company were all in position and had everything they needed, exchanging smiles and a friendly word. He knew most of them well, though they had received several new recruits in the past few days with whom obviously he was less familiar. He stopped by one lad he didn't recognize who was sitting cleaning his rifle. He looked about 16 years old, though was probably older. Oliver stopped in front of him.

"What's your name, lad?" The boy stiffened to attention.

"Barnes, sir. Private Barnes."

"Stand easy, Barnes." He smiled at him. "Welcome to the sharp end! Everything alright?"

"Aye, sir. Grand, sir. Thank you, sir."

"Good lad!" said Oliver. "Carry on." And he moved on down the trench. As he returned to his own position, the battalion HQ runner appeared.

"Colonel Sinclair's compliments, sir, all company commanders to his dug-out in 15 minutes." He hurried away. Oliver had a word with the sergeant-major and then made his own way along the trench. He was careful to keep his head below the parapet – he was well aware that, at least during day-light hours, there were likely to be enemy snipers hidden not far away, waiting for some incautious soldier to come into view, even if only for a moment, and they didn't often miss! One advantage of their side having occupied the same trench for a couple of weeks was that they had been able to construct quite a decent parapet out of sandbags, so that progress along the duckboards was a little less hazardous, always assuming you weren't too tall. One man in his company, Private Tompkins, stood over six foot four, and his mates used to joke that he was a great gauge of the enemy's preparedness: send 'Lofty' along the trench, and if he didn't get shot at, there probably wasn't anybody out there!

Oliver was the first to the CO's dugout, but his fellow company-commanders were not far behind him. As he looked about him, he reflected wryly that he was, by a fair margin in most cases, the oldest man there. Even the CO, Lt-Col Peter Sinclair, was his junior by a couple of years. Had it not been for the severe bout of dysentery that had sent him, first to the field hospital, and then back to England to recover, which took him out of the action for a couple of months, he might well have been in Sinclair's position. It was not something he ever regretted. While the job might have been marginally safer, he did not crave the greater responsibility for men's lives which would have inevitably have been his. No doubt it would be his lot sometime, but not yet!

"Right, chaps," said the CO when all were gathered, "it will come as no surprise to you that we are going to make a push tomorrow, weather permitting, which I feel sure it will." He indicated a large map which was pegged to the rough table in the middle of his dug-out.

"The plan is to push Fritz back on a fairly narrow front to create a salient from which we can enfilade his defences on either side of us which will force him to withdraw on a much wider scale. We've got the middle, and we have the Canadians on the right and the Highlanders on the left, so I don't think we need to worry about being enfiladed ourselves!" There was a murmur of approval. The fighting qualities of the Scots and the Canadians were legendary, and no-one minded going into battle with them by their side. Sinclair pointed to the map.

"As you can see, the German front line is not far away, as little as 400 yards in some places, and their second line is about 200 yards beyond that. Our battalion will be first over and our initial objective is the Hun's front line trenches. Once we are in position there, 4th Battalion will advance through us and take the second line. When they have that under control, we will move forward to join them and consolidate there to repel any counter-attack. We will then get further orders. It shouldn't be too hard. The gunners are going to put a hell of a barrage on the two enemy lines from 05.00 hours, so the wire should be broken up and the enemy in no position to resist you. The barrage is due to lift at 07.00 so that is when we jump the bags. Signals will be right behind you laying line so that by the time you reach your objective you should be able to communicate with us back here. Any questions?"

"What if we're stopped short of our objective?" The speaker

was Captain Meek, newly-promoted, ludicrously young, and still a bit short of confidence.

"You won't be!" said Sinclair firmly. "It's going to be a huge bombardment. I'd be surprised if we encounter a lot of resistance before we get to their first line. Anything else? Good! Let's synchronise watches." They all did this.

"Alright, that's it chaps. Good luck! See you in Berlin!" They all emerged from the bunker and Oliver made his way back to his company's position to brief his officers.

§

The next day dawned cool and dry. There would probably have been, as usual, some residual mist drifting over the ground but it was hard to tell because it had been obliterated by the shelling. Oliver had forgotten how terrifying and awe-inspiring a concentrated bombardment was, even when it was directed at the unfortunate enemy and not yourselves. There seemed no relief from the screaming of the shells as they ripped through the air overhead and the thumping crashes as they exploded a short way ahead. There was some artillery fire in response from the German side but it was spasmodic and mainly ill-directed, and no shells landed in their sector. As the jump-off time approached, Oliver had a last tour of his company's position to make sure everybody was ready. He passed Private Barnes, standing next to the ladder he was about to shin up. He looked, and no doubt was, absolutely terrified. Oliver paused beside him.

"Alright, Barnes?" The boy nodded and licked his lips nervously.

"Aye, sir."

"Good lad. You'll be fine. Just keep on going straight ahead. You'll be there before you know it."

"Thank you, sir." Oliver patted the boy on his shoulder and gave him a smile before moving on.

Back in his position, he looked intently at his watch as the hands moved slowly towards seven o'clock. At two minutes before, the gunfire suddenly ceased. Damn! Why? What had happened? They should have been firing up to the last second. He raised the whistle to his lips and paused it there. They needed to all go together. He watched in agony as the second hand wound slowly round the face. At one minute to, someone's nerve obviously broke and he heard a whistle blow down the line. He blew his own with all his might and shouted as loudly as he could, "Right lads! Up we go! Charge!"

The soldier next to him scrambled up the ladder over the parapet and Oliver followed him, drawing his pistol as he emerged onto the ground beyond. For the first few seconds there was very little fire but then he heard the staccato rattle of a machine gun and a crackle of rifles. The soldier in front of him suddenly dropped soundlessly to the ground and lay there quite still as Oliver passed by. To his left and right he could see a long line of men jogging steadily forward, rifles at the ready with bayonets fixed. The ground before him was rough and torn up and once he had to skirt round a large shell crater, half filled with rain water, and stifle his natural instinct to take refuge in it.

They were nearing the German line now and he could see the flashes from the defenders' weapons. Twice he could feel the rush of bullets as they passed by close to his face. Then he heard the shriek of an approaching shell and knew in an instant that it was landing very close. "Down, men!" he shouted as he flung himself face down into the dirt. Within a second there was a shocking concussion and he felt his whole body being smashed from the left. And then he was aware of nothing more.

§

When Oliver regained consciousness, everything seemed grey. His whole body was gripped in a grey cloak of pain and he could see nothing but grey before him. He soon realized that this was because he was lying on his back looking at the sky. He became aware of movement beneath him and the occasional jar which sent shards of acute pain lancing through the ache that enveloped him and caused him to cry out involuntarily.

"Sorry, chum! We'll soon have you there." He realized that he was being carried along on a stretcher. The man at his front had a broad back with a red cross on his armband just visible. He couldn't see the man behind him who had just spoken. He felt another deep stab of pain and then lost consciousness again.

When he came to once more, there was no sense of motion and he realized he was resting on the ground. There was still the grey sky overhead, but around him there was a bustle, orders being given and people moving around. The pain had, thankfully, subsided to a dull ache. It had been replaced by an overwhelming lassitude. He lay there completely exhausted, lacking either the will or the capacity to move any part of his body. He closed his eyes. After a short while he heard somebody say "Major! Can you hear me?" He opened his eyes and saw a man standing over him. He wore the insignia of a captain and a red cross arm-band. He looked desperately tired.

"How are you feeling?"

"Sore," croaked Oliver. The man smiled.

"Not surprised! I'm Dr Bates and I've given you something for the pain so that should help. We're going to move you back to the base hospital so they can do something about your leg."

"Thanks." Oliver wondered vaguely what needed to be done about his leg but simply lacked the energy to ask.

"Good man," said the doctor. "Try not to worry. You're going to be fine."

Oliver would later remember the journey from the first aid post to the hospital as among the most disagreeable experiences of his life. He and several other gravely wounded soldiers were loaded into a high-sided cart which then proceeded very slowly along what was evidently an extremely uneven road. The journey lasted several hours and whatever pain-killer he had been given wore off before too long, so that every lurch and bump of the cart was agony. One of the other soldiers groaned and screamed for virtually the whole time. Long before they got where they were going, Oliver felt exhausted, drained, and hopeless. If someone had walked up with a loaded gun and offered to put him out of his misery, he would have accepted.

At last, however, the cart came to a halt. They had obviously reached their destination. The back of the cart was lowered and Oliver and his companions were unloaded and carried into a tent. As he was placed gently on the ground there, Oliver passed out again. When he came to once more some time later, he saw the most amazing and beautiful sight.

"Molly!" The sight of his sister standing beside his stretcher, looking down at him worriedly, lifted his spirits in a way he could not have imagined. The pain was still intense, but he felt he could bear anything.

Molly knelt down beside him and took his hand in both of hers. "How are you feeling, Olly?"

"Pretty sore." He tried to chuckle but it came out as a groan.

"Have they given you any morphine?"

"I think I got some at the first aid post. Probably not since then. I'm not really sure."

She got to her feet and walked briskly away, returning soon with a syringe. She rolled back the right sleeve of his tunic and emptied the contents of the syringe into his arm.

"That should help. Give it a couple of minutes." She looked down at her brother and shook her head.

"You cannot imagine, Olly, how I have been dreading this."

"What d'you mean?" though he knew, of course.

"Coming in to the hospital one day, looking down on a stretcher, and seeing you! Still, at least you're alive!"

"Do you know what's the matter with me? Everything down my left side feels sore, but especially my leg. And I can't seem to move my left arm."

"I think your leg is the main thing," she replied. "It looks badly smashed up. Doctor should be along to have a look at you soon."

She sighed.

"I must go. I have other patients to see to, but I'll be back as soon as I can. Don't go anywhere!" And she disappeared. Oliver lay back and closed his eyes. The throbbing pain in his leg was still there, but somewhat duller. The drug was evidently starting to work. He felt the stirrings of hope.

§

It was probably half an hour before the doctor arrived, a balding, slightly untidy, rubicund man of middle age with rimless spectacles. The spectacles, like their owner, looked a bit unkempt, held together with a strip of surgical tape. The lines around his mouth and eyes suggested he normally did a lot of smiling. He was not smiling now. He examined Oliver thoroughly from top to toe, gently palpating the painful areas on the left leg and arm. When he had finished he wiped his hands on a cloth and looked down at Oliver.

"Major ..?"

"Nayland. Oliver Nayland."

"Major Nayland! You have a broken arm, nothing complicated, looks like a clean break of the humerus. We should be able to fix that. Your leg is a mess though. Smashed in several places I would say. I won't really know what can be done until we have a closer look. And I won't be doing that while you're awake. You know, you're a very lucky young man. With those injuries it is amazing you did not sever an artery and if you had, you'd have bled to death in no time." He smiled for the first time. "Your hour is not yet at hand!"

"When are you going to operate?" Oliver asked.

"Soon as possible," the doctor replied. "No point wasting time. The quicker we do it, the less chance of infection. I'll be back with you shortly." He was as good as his word, reappearing quite a short time later with a middle–aged nurse and two medical orderlies. The orderlies picked up Oliver's stretcher and moved him to an adjacent tent, where they transferred him, as gently as possible but still somewhat painfully, onto a padded rectangular bench about waist high, which evidently served as the operating table. The area was screened off from the rest of the tent by a sheet suspended from a line running across the tent, presumably to prevent the other occupants of the tent from being discouraged by what was going on in there!

Once the doctor was satisfied that Oliver was properly in place, he turned to him.

"Now, Major, we're going to see what we can do about your leg. I'm Doctor Simkins and this is Sister Redman who is going to be helping me. First thing we'll do is to knock you out so you don't give us a lot of lip while we're working. I want you to just lie back, try and relax and breathe as normally as possible. Sister will put this cloth over your face and we'll drop some chloroform onto it which should make you a bit woozy at first and then send you off to sleep. We'll keep dripping ether onto the cloth as we go so you don't wake up before we're finished. All right?"

"Thanks, doctor. The pain is really quite bad, now, Is there anything you can do about that?"

"Don't worry, old chap. You won't feel a thing soon, and when we're done I'll give you another shot of morphine." The doctor nodded to Sister Redman who moved forward with a folded cloth and a bottle of liquid.

§

When Oliver awoke, a good deal of time had passed. Outside the tent it was evidently dark and the light inside it was provided by lanterns. He was back on ground level again. He could not move his left arm and did not even try to move his legs, but the pain had at least subsided to a dull ache. His mouth was very dry. He was able to attract the attention of a passing orderly to request some water and soon after that a nurse appeared with a jug and lifted his head up so he could drink. While he was doing this,

Sister Redman appeared. She had a kind, sympathetic face that reminded him of his mother. She too looked very tired.

"Good evening, Major. How are you feeling?"

"Not too bad. A bit sore. How did it go?"

She didn't answer at first but knelt down and adjusted the blankets that had been draped over him.

"Well, we've mended the arm. That was a nice clean break and it should heal well." She paused.

"But your leg was very badly smashed up, I'm afraid. There was just nothing the doctor could do and there was a very high risk of infection, so he had to remove most of it." Her voice had a gentle West Country burr.

For a moment, Oliver wasn't sure he had understood.

"D'you mean you've amputated my leg?"

"Yes, I'm afraid so. It really was the only thing to do. I'm so sorry. Dr Simkins would have told you himself but he has had to go and get some sleep. He's been on duty for over two days."

Oliver lay there, speechless, while the nurse checked the dressings on his arm and his leg. It was hard to digest what he had just been told. He had occasionally watched while wounded soldiers were loaded onto the train to take them to the ferry and away to England and had looked with pity at the men swinging by on crutches to make up for the absence of a lower limb. Now he was to be among them.

"Has my sister been around?" he asked. "Nurse Nayland, Molly Nayland?"

"Yes," replied Sister Redman. "She came just after we had finished. You were still unconscious. She had to go back to work. I'm sure she'll be here to see you soon. I think she is still on duty."

It wasn't very long after that Molly herself did appear. She too looked very tired and her apron was grimy and stained. She knelt down beside him and seized his right hand in both of hers.

"How are you?"

"I'm fine." He smiled."But I think that dream of playing rugger for England is gone!"

"Oh Olly!" She squeezed his hand and her voice broke. "I am so, so sorry! Dr Simkins is a wonderful surgeon. He will have done everything he could, I know it."

"I'm sure he did, Moll, it's just one of those things." He spoke to comfort her, but perhaps hoped that he might convince himself as well. "You mustn't worry about me. At least I'm still alive!"

"Yes, at least you're still alive." She wiped her eyes and stood up. "I must go back. They've just brought in another batch of wounded. I expect they'll be moving you out soon. We need the space."

"What, to another hospital?"

"Well, yes, but soon back home. I promise I'll be back to see you before you go. I have something very important to tell you."

"Really? What is that?"

"I'll tell you when I see you," said Molly firmly. "Au revoir, my darling." And she was gone.

Oliver lay back, trying to ignore the throbbing pain that had resumed in his leg or rather, he reflected wryly, where his leg used to be. He could not remember his younger sister ever calling him 'darling'! It was a funny old world.

§

It was probably not more than an hour later that a nurse came by to give him another syringe of painkillers and tell him that he was about to be moved out. She didn't know where he would be going.

"My sister's working in this hospital" said Oliver. "Nurse Nayland. She was very keen to see me before I left. Can you get a message to her?" The nurse said she'd see what she could do and hurried away. Very few minutes had passed before Molly appeared again and knelt beside him.

"Oliver, I've only got a few moments, so please listen carefully to me. It's about Ruth."

"Humphrey's Ruth?"

"Of course Humphrey's Ruth!" She gently laid her finger on his lips. "Just listen!"

CHAPTER THIRTEEN

RUTH

There was not a town in Britain where a visitor would not have known there was a war on, and York was no different in this. The number of men in uniform walking the streets, the newspaper billboards screaming the battle headlines, the chat in the pubs and clubs, all told the story. Ruth knew hardly anyone who did not have a son or brother or cousin serving somewhere, in France, or Mesopotamia, or Africa, or with the navy on the dangerous seas. The city had largely managed, however, to maintain a detachment from the actual conflict itself. There had been that afternoon in the first winter of the war when a squadron of the German navy had shelled the coastal towns of Scarborough and Whitby, and like everybody she had read with horror of the civilians killed and seen pictures in the paper of the shattered buildings.

Even those stories, though, seemed remote to the peaceful streets of the old city of York. All that had changed one evening earlier that year when Ruth and her aunt had been sitting in the parlour enjoying a cup of tea before retiring to bed. Little Elizabeth had only just gone to sleep. Then just over a year old, she was teething and unusually fractious, and both women were gratefully enjoying a few minutes of repose.

Suddenly they heard a distant crash and boom, and the gas lights flickered and then went out altogether. This was followed by further booms in the distance. She and Aunt Mary rushed out into the street. Without the lamps it was quite dark, but there was a glow of fires in the distance and, as they stood there, they could hear, and even feel, the concussion of more explosions.

The next morning they learned, with the rest of York, that a German Zeppelin airship had swooped low over the city, bombing indiscriminately and leaving a trail of destruction. Several people had been killed and many others injured. Later in the day, Ruth had pushed Elizabeth in her pram down to Nunnery Lane where she had seen the results of the bombing. She marveled at the broken houses and the huge craters in the road. In a strange way, although very sorry for those directly affected, she felt almost glad that the war had come to York. It somehow brought her closer to those she knew who were fighting. In particular she felt it got her closer to Humphrey.

Those first few months after he left he had lived in her thoughts. She had written to him every week, and received several letters in response. When she left Cowdenhall to come to York, though, all that had changed. The flow of letters from Humphrey had stopped abruptly. For a while she had continued writing, although she no longer knew to what address she should send them. She kept her letters to him together in a box under her bed until, shortly before Elizabeth was born, in a fit of misery and despair, she had burned them all. She would sometimes glean fragments of news about him passed on to Aunt Mary by Emily, so she knew he was alive.

The trauma of her baby's birth, and the sheer exhaustion of caring for her in its aftermath had to some degree thrust him to the back of her mind, but he did not stay there for long. This was not least because every time she looked into her daughter's tiny face she could see him there. She had heard it said that babies usually resemble their fathers to begin with, a protective characteristic from primitive days when the father of the family needed to be encouraged not to throw this noisy little interloper out of the cave. And it was true of Elizabeth. Her eyes were his, the shape of her chin, the set of her ears. So much of her personality too reminded

Ruth of Humphrey. She was a sunny, cheerful little thing, seldom strident or demanding, and she inspired great affection in those about her. Aunt Mary, a practical, no-nonsense woman, was besotted, and even her son Edward, as self-centred and anti-social as most lads his age, seldom failed to pick her up and hug her when he came in from work. Aunt Mary's very grumpy old cat, a one-eyed, black and white, neutered tom appropriately called Nelson, would permit her to take liberties with him which he would not tolerate from anybody else, and never tried to bite or scratch her. If her attentions became too much, he would simply get up and move out of range.

Late one morning Ruth was returning from an expedition to the baker for bread and the butcher for a leg of lamb. She was quite used, by now, to purchasing provisions from the shops, rather than making them or obtaining them from your own field or kitchen garden. She had read of people queuing for groceries in the south, but in York supply and demand were still fairly well balanced and you seldom had to wait long. As she pushed the pram round the corner into the road where her aunt's house was, she suddenly stopped, shocked into immobility. Half-way down the road, opposite their house, a soldier was standing in the street. His face was turned away and she couldn't see it and for a moment she was seized with the thrilling possibility. Almost immediately, she dismissed it. It could not be him. Anyway, the figure was too tall. She walked on and as she got nearer she could see that the man was on crutches. There was something familiar about him. He heard the rattle of the pram and turned to face her which was when she saw with shock that he had only one leg. A second after she had noticed this, she recognized the face under the peaked cap.

"Master Oliver!"

"Hullo, Ruth." Oliver smiled down at her. "Excuse me not shaking hands!"

"Oh! Master Oliver! What happened to your leg?" What a really stupid question!

"Had a bit of an argument with a German shell – the leg came off second best. And can we drop the 'Master'? Unless you want me to call you 'Mistress Ruth'?"

"No, of course not! But … how did you find us?"

"Molly told me – but don't worry! She hasn't told anyone else and nor have I. She saw me in hospital just before I was sent back. She very much wants me to talk to you."

Ruth considered this in silence for a few seconds, then said "Aye, well, you'd best come in." She turned and led the way into the house.

Elizabeth had been dozing on the way back from the shops, but the talking had woken her and she stood up in the pram, demanding to be taken out. Ruth waved Oliver into the little front sitting room and lifted her daughter up and followed him in. He lowered himself awkwardly into an armchair. Ruth sat opposite, with Elizabeth clinging to her knees, round-eyed and in awe of this oddly-dressed stranger.

"Ruth, she's beautiful!"

"Aye," said Ruth, stroking her child's curly head. "She's a bonny bantling. Lizzie, this is your Uncle Oliver." She met Oliver's gaze. "Why did Molly tell you? Why have you come?" She suddenly felt a sharp stab of fear. "Is it about Humphrey? Has something happened to him?"

"Humphrey's fine, as far as we know," he reassured her. "We haven't heard from him for a while, but that's normal. It takes weeks for letters to come from Africa. We'd have been told if there was anything wrong." He paused for a moment. "But it is about Humphrey, in a way. Molly thinks, and I agree with her, that it's time Humphrey knew about..." he waved at the toddler, "about Lizzie."

Ruth didn't speak for a while and they sat in silence. Then she said "Would you care for a cuppa?"

"That would be nice, thank you," he replied. "You get quite addicted to tea in the army!"

Ruth got up and went out to the kitchen at the back, the little girl following her. The stove was still burning from breakfast and it did not take many minutes to fill the kettle and put it on the hob. While she was waiting for the water to boil she had a chance to think about what Oliver had said. In her dreams she had seen herself, holding Elizabeth by the hand, down at the railway station, waiting at the barrier as the returning troops poured off the train. Amid them all she would suddenly spy Humphrey, bare-headed and smiling, his kit-bag over his shoulder, walking down the platform towards them. Their eyes would meet and in a moment they'd be in each others' arms.

"And who is this?" she'd hear him say, smiling down at the little girl beside her.

"This is Elizabeth. This is your daughter."

And in her fantasy he would kneel down and embrace his child, then lift her up and hold them both to him. In her mind she had determined that he would not be burdened with the knowledge until that time. What was different now that could change that?

She poured the boiling water from the kettle into the tea pot and placed it with two cups and saucers and a small jug of milk on a tray which she carried through to the sitting room, Lizzie still doggedly hanging onto her dress. She placed it on the dresser by the wall where it was out of reach of the child and poured them both a cup.

She sat down again opposite Oliver and Lizzie climbed onto her lap.

"When did that happen?" She nodded towards his leg.

"About two months ago. They shipped me back very quickly, but I've been in a hospital in Dover since then. They had to make sure the leg wasn't infected. Also, I had broken my arm so that was all plastered up." He smiled. "Bit difficult with crutches if you can only use one arm!"

Ruth grimaced sympathetically. "Does it still hurt?"

"Not much now. I used to feel pain in my leg even though it wasn't there any more, but that hardly ever happens now."

"Will they give you a new leg?"

"So they tell me! Apparently they have to wait for the old one to heal completely and all the swelling to go down before than can fit it. Meanwhile, I'm getting pretty good with these crutches! I'm going to end up with very strong arms!" He made a mock-ferocious face at Lizzie. "I shall be able to crack chestnuts with my hands!" The child smiled uncertainly.

Ruth looked steadily across the room at Oliver.

"I expect Molly told you, I don't want Humphrey bothered with this until he comes home. There's nowt he can do. It'll just be another thing he must bide. I haven't heard from him for nigh on two years. Happen he's forgotten us."

"I can promise you he hasn't. He asks after you every time he writes to Molly. I'm not sure if he still writes to you, but Molly said he kept on for a long time after he stopped receiving letters from you. Perhaps your father didn't pass his letters on?" Ruth didn't say anything. That was all too possible.

"Ruth, don't you think Humphrey has a right to know? I've no doubt at all that he loves you very much. It might be a bit of a shock when he finds out about Lizzie, but when he gets used to the idea, he'll be tickled pink. It'll give him one more thing to look forward to."

Oliver took a large mouthful of tea.

"And there's another thing. If Lizzie is accepted by Humphrey, which I am quite sure she will be, and by the rest of our family, which I think Molly and I can guarantee, then it will be much harder for your father to ignore her. Wouldn't it be better for everybody if he were to come around?"

Ruth didn't say anything for a minute or two while she digested this. What Oliver said made sense. She felt a sensation of peace and relief steal over her.

"All right," she said at last, "but I must be the one to tell him. If I write a letter, can you make sure it gets to him?"

"With pleasure! Mother will know where to send it. I'll enclose it with a letter from me. I haven't been home yet. They don't know I'm coming so I think it'll be a nice surprise. Mary Elizabeth wanted to visit me in Dover but I managed to put her off." He chuckled grimly. "Hospitals like that are not pleasant places."

Ruth got up from her chair.

"Lizzie needs her dinner. Happen you can feed her while I write the letter?"

Oliver and Elizabeth transferred to the kitchen where Ruth sat the toddler down in front of a bowl of bread and milk and told her firmly that Mam was busy but Uncle Oliver was going to feed her. Lizzie was uncertain at first, but hunger got the better of shyness and Ruth was able to leave them to it while she went back to the sitting room to write the most important letter of her life.

After half an hour or so, Ruth returned to the kitchen to see that all barriers were down. The bowl was empty and the little girl was giggling delightedly while she reached up to grab hold of Oliver's moustaches.

"Mind out, love. I'm sure Uncle Oliver doesn't want you pulling his beard!"

Oliver laughed. "Uncle Oliver doesn't mind you pulling his beard any time you like." He reached over and tousled her hair.

"Here's the letter," Ruth said, and Oliver took it and tucked into the inside pocket of his jacket.

"I'll see it gets off as soon as possible," he promised as he levered himself to his feet. Ruth accompanied him the door.

"When's your train?" she asked.

"I think there's one about 3.00 o'clock. I need to pick up my bag from the ticket office and I'll get my ticket then. I should have plenty of time. Thank you for the tea."

"It was our pleasure," Ruth said. She looked gravely up at him. "Thank you for coming. I'm glad you did."

"So am I," said Oliver. "So am I." On an impulse Ruth leant forward and kissed him gently on the cheek.

"Goodbye," she said. "I hope we see you again soon."

"I am quite sure you will! Goodbye. 'Bye little one." Oliver smiled down at Lizzie and blew her a kiss. Then he swiveled around and made his way off up the road.

Ruth watched until he disappeared from view round the corner and then she turned and went inside. She felt a deeper contentment than she had for many months.

CHAPTER FOURTEEN

MOLLY

Molly had, quite fortuitously, been able to get home for a few days very soon after Oliver had arrived there. The onset of winter had brought the conflict on the Western Front grinding to something of a halt. Although there was still a steady stream of broken bodies flowing back behind the lines, the appalling volume was no longer there and it was a good opportunity to give the medical staff some of the rest that they richly deserved and desperately needed. As Molly sat in the warm and comfortable compartment of the train as it made its way through the winter gloom and rain, she felt mentally and physically drained. She had a feeling that as soon as she passed through the front door of the vicarage she might simply collapse in a heap. However, there was one important thing which, with Oliver's help, she was going to need to do without delay, and she would have to hold herself together until she had done it.

The train was a few minutes late – it had been late leaving York – and as they pulled into the station could see the familiar silhouette of her father on the platform sheltering under a large umbrella.

She got down from the train with her bag. She was the only person alighting at Cowdenhall. In the dim light of the late afternoon, she could not see his face, but her father's greeting embrace seemed stronger, less formal, than it usually was. Aubrey carried her bag and she took charge of the umbrella. She put her arm through his and squeezed it.

"How are you? How's Mother?"

"We're both well. Your mother has had a bit of a cold, but she seems quite recovered now. Dizzy is in good form. He'll be delighted to see you!"

"And Oliver? How is he?"

Her father sighed.

"Well, we haven't seen a great deal of him yet. He's staying with the Baths, of course. He seems rather quiet and introspective, not really like himself. Poor chap! What a terrible thing to have happened to him."

"Yes, it was," said Molly firmly, "but at least he is alive, and he will never have to go back to that awful place."

"Well, that is true. As Livy tells us, we are slower to recognize blessings than misfortunes. Life is going to be very difficult for him, though."

"Yes it will, but we can all help him deal with it."

"Oliver says you saw him in France soon after he was wounded?"

"Yes, I did." Her mind went back fleetingly to the tented ward at St Omer, and she could see again the rows of broken bodies, many dead or dying, hear the cries and groans of the wounded, and smell the blood, urine, and disinfectant. She was very thankful that her parents could have no understanding of what it was like there.

"How is Mary coping?"

"Look, quite well, as far as one can tell. She's a sweet girl, you know, and obviously devoted to Oliver. They are all coming round for dinner this evening".

"Oh, that'll be lovely!" With everybody there, it would clearly not be an opportune time for her and Oliver to carry out their mission. Another occasion would have to be arranged.

By now they were walking up the path to the front door. Molly glanced up at her father's face, now illuminated by the light from the porch window. He looked much older than she remembered.

Impulsively she hugged his arm and reached up to give him a kiss on the cheek.

"Dear Father! It is so good to be home!"

§

The reunions inside the house were heartening. Her mother had embraced her with great warmth.

"Oh, Molly! How wonderful to see you again! But you've lost weight! We shall have to fatten you up!" She beamed at her daughter with transparent joy. The welcome from Dizzy had been no less joyful though a good deal less complicated. The little dog had a single-minded devotion to all the important humans in his life, and the more of them there were present, the happier he was.

Molly excused herself presently so that she could have a leisurely bath before dinner. As she lay in the water, luxuriating in its heavenly warmth for the first time in months, she thought about how she was going to broach the subject of Ruth and the baby with her parents. For everybody's sake it was vital that she should get their unequivocal support. She knew that the idea of an illegitimate child in the family would be repugnant to them and would offend their Christian values and sense of propriety. But she also knew that they were compassionate, loving, and intelligent people. They would need, she reasoned, little persuasion of the importance of Christian forgiveness, and of doing what was best for all the people they loved. That they loved their children deeply was beyond any possible doubt. And they knew them well. It would not be hard to convince them that Humphrey, whatever sins he might have committed, remained a decent, upright person who deserved their continuing support. She was confident of being able to encourage a similar attitude to Ruth, beginning from the basis of "if she's good enough for him, she's good enough for us."

She was certain that it would be best for her and Oliver to make a joint approach. Probably best, too, not to beat about the bush. In any case, she reflected, it was something of a relief not to have to grasp this particular nettle tonight. She could give herself up to the pleasures of a family gathering. She was so looking forward to seeing Oliver again!

§

The dinner party was as jovial and relaxing as she could have hoped. The Baths, senior, were cheerful and friendly as always, and Mary was her usual serene self. Molly was most pleasantly surprised with Oliver. Although he still looked thin and drawn, those few days back had relaxed him greatly, and there was a trace of the old sparkle in his demeanor. They did not speak of the war at all. The only Bath family member absent was Hector. On the outbreak of war he, like thousands of other young men, had gone straight to the nearest recruiting office to sign up. Unlike most of them however, he had been rejected – the medical examination revealing a heart murmur that rendered him unfit for military service. In the excitement and euphoria of the time, this had been a bitter blow to Hector, although, Molly knew well, a source of profound relief to his mother. To try and lessen the blow, George had used his contacts to find Hector a government position in the area of munitions and supply in London, where he now was. Molly was aware that he had made at least one more, equally unsuccessful, attempt to enlist.

The cooking staff at the Vicarage (Mother and Mrs Plumtree) might not have been capable of quite the level of sophistication available at the Bath's table, but it was still a delicious and satisfying meal, and contrasted more than favourably with anything Molly had enjoyed in recent weeks. Watching Mary with her brother, she was glad to see a genuine concern and care evident. She was surprised, though, at what seemed a greater confidence in his wife. Perhaps she felt more certain of him now that his dependence on her was so much more than it had been. Molly hoped that Mary would have the good sense not to overplay that particular hand. She knew her brother well enough to realize that he would keenly resent his loss of independence, and would not look well upon those who might seek to exploit it in any way. All being well, Mary's love for him, of which Molly had no doubt, would lead her away from that particular pitfall.

They did not stay up late. Oliver said that his leg was a bit sore and Molly was, by this stage, so tired she could hardly speak coherently. As they were preparing to leave she had a chance to talk to her brother alone.

"How did you go, with Ruth?" she asked.

"I managed to persuade her that this cat should be let out of the bag," he replied. "She wanted to be the one to tell Humphrey so she wrote me a letter for him which I sent off with one of mine yesterday. I told her we would be talking to Mother and Father."

"Oh! I'm so glad! Can you come over tomorrow, so we can speak to them?" she asked.

"Should be able to. I'll get Jenkins to drop me round. About ten-ish?" Jenkins was the Bath's chauffeur.

"I'm sure that'll be fine," Molly said. "I'll tell them you're coming in the morning. If we need to change anything, I'll telephone." She looked up at him. "It's just wonderful to see you, Ollie, and you're looking so well!" She opened the door for him and they walked out into the hall where the others were putting on their coats. She said her farewells to the Baths and Mary and exchanged a brief goodnight kiss with her parents. Back up in her room she had hardly got the energy to change into her nightdress and she was asleep almost before her head hit the pillow.

§

Jenkins delivered Oliver promptly at ten o'clock and Molly met him at the front door.

"Mary was keen to come too," he said as he levered himself over the threshold into the hall, "so I had to tell her that it was private family business we needed to discuss. I think she was a bit miffed at being left out. I promised I'd be back for lunch."

Louisa bustled happily about getting them all tea and scones, freshly baked by Mrs Plumtree, and they settled comfortably in the sitting room. When they were all sitting down, Molly spoke.

"Mother, Father, Ollie and I have something to tell you."

"Goodness me, what can that be?" said Louisa in some alarm.

"Don't worry, mother, it's nothing bad. In fact, it's rather wonderful." She paused to collect herself.

"You have a grand-daughter!"

Both parents looked at her in amazement.

"A grand-daughter?" said Aubrey incredulously. "What do you mean?"

"You remember Ruth, Ruth Moffat?"

"Oh, yes," said Louisa. "Albert's daughter. Nice girl. Humphrey's friend. We haven't seen her for ages. I think she had to go to York to look after her aunt."

"Yes," said Molly, "well, it wasn't quite like that. She and Humphrey were more than just friends. Before he left … well, something happened. She became pregnant. When Albert found out, he sent her to York to stay with his wife's sister. The baby was born there. She's a little girl and her name is Elizabeth."

The vicar and his wife lay back on the sofa where they were seated, struck dumb with astonishment. They looked at their two children sitting solemnly before them.

Aubrey found his voice first.

"How long have you known?"

"I've known for a while," replied Molly. "I ran into Ruth by accident in York when I was back on leave last year. She made me promise not to tell anybody "

"And what about you, Oliver?" asked his mother.

"I found out quite recently. Molly visited me in hospital after I was wounded and, knowing I'd be sent home, asked me to see Ruth and try and persuade her to tell Humphrey."

"You mean he knows nothing about this."

"No. That was Ruth's main reason for wanting to keep it all secret. She didn't want Humphrey to be worried about it while he couldn't do anything." Oliver paused. "I stopped off in York on the way here and saw Ruth and met little Elizabeth. I was able to persuade Ruth that the time had come to tell everybody. I posted off a letter for her to Humphrey yesterday."

Molly went on to explain the circumstances of Ruth's exile, how her father insisted on the child being given up for adoption, and his refusal to accept her back.

"I did think it was odd that we hadn't seen her back here for so long," said Louisa, "and that would also explain the change in Albert's attitude – you were saying just the other day, Aubrey, that he has been so much more distant with you in the past year or so. Now we know why."

Molly looked steadily at her parents.

"I know this must be shock for you both. What Humphrey and Ruth did was wrong, perhaps even sinful. But they aren't bad people – quite the contrary. What's happened has happened. Both Ollie and I," she glanced at her brother, "feel so strongly that we ought to do everything we can to make the best of it instead of," she gestured with her hand, "this foolishness, with people kept apart by a miserable secret."

Oliver leaned forward, steadying himself with the armrest of Molly's chair.

"I told you I had met Ruth and Elizabeth in York this week. She is such a beautiful little girl, Mother. You will adore her."

Some moments passed when no-one spoke. Aubrey and Louisa sat with eyes downcast. Then Aubrey raised his head, looked across at his wife and cleared his throat.

"Well, there's no use pretending that this hasn't all been a terrible shock. One never imagines this sort of thing happening in one's own family. But so much has happened in the past couple of years that we could never have imagined. So many fine young men dead or torn apart, you two going off to experience awful things, you," he gestured to Oliver, "making such a grave sacrifice. The poet tells us 'Be bold! Take courage and be strong of soul!' I can only speak for myself here and I'm sure that if your mother disagrees with me she will say so." He glanced across again at Louisa and fiddled with his spectacles.

"I feel that if Humphrey has had the courage to go to a savage land so far away to fight for all we hold dear, then we should have the courage to accept his little family among us and mind them for him." Louisa reached across and held his hand.

"I do not disagree with a word, my dear."

On hearing these words, Molly sprang up and knelt before her parents, grasping them both by the hand.

"Thank you for understanding, thank you for ..." and then the high emotion of the moment, on top of the strain of the past many months, got the better of her and she burst into tears.

§

After much use of a hanky, some heartfelt hugs among the female members of the party, and rather more restrained back-patting from the males, two generations of Naylands settled down to plan the practicalities of dealing with the next one.

"They ought to come and live with us," said Louisa. "Do you think she'd want to do that?"

"I'm sure she would," said Molly. "I dare say her aunt will miss them both, but I would think she will also be grateful to have two less mouths to feed. I can go into York and see her."

"Before we do that," said her father firmly, "we must sort things out with Albert Moffat. You can leave that to me. As the poet tells us, 'words will not fail when the matter is well considered'."

"I'll come with you, Father," said Oliver. "Jenkins is coming back with the motor in about an hour's time and he can take us both round to the farm. I think it might help if Albert saw me beside you." Aubrey looked at his son while he considered this.

"I think you're right, Oliver," he said at length. "That would be a good idea. Thank you."

"And when Humphrey comes home," said Louisa, "they can be wed."

'Indeed they can," said her husband. "Let us pray for that!"

166

CHAPTER FIFTEEN

HUMPHREY

Life in the African bush, Humphrey had come to realize, had many very disagreeable aspects – the heat, the countless unpleasant insects, some merely annoying, some a threat to health, the occasional encounters with dangerous and unpredictable animals, the roughness of the terrain, the lack of the most basic amenities that civilized people considered essential. On the other hand, there were some compensations. Wakening in the soft, warm, stillness of the African dawn, with the sun starting to colour the sky in the East and the cool dew underfoot, was always beautiful, if you allowed yourself to think about it. Sometimes Humphrey did allow himself to think about it.

They were camped near the banks of a stream flowing through what was, theoretically at least, Portuguese territory. Vorbeck and his men had been painfully driven south through German East Africa and should have been trapped between the British forces and a string of Portuguese garrisons along the border. However, as Humphrey's CO had sardonically observed, the soldiers manning these garrisons had varied from completely hopeless to absolutely useless and had offered little or no resistance to the battle-hardened German askaris. They had no difficulty in slicing through the border line and penetrating deep into the heart of the Portuguese colony, with the British forces, including Humphrey and his men in, if not hot, at least warm pursuit. They had seen not a sign of the enemy for several weeks, if you discounted the empty food stores and resentful local inhabitants that they had left in their wake, which did not render the British advance any easier. The only saving grace was the end of the rains, which had vastly improved the state of the tracks they had to negotiate, and reduced to manageable trickles the streams they had to cross.

Humphrey went round the sentry posts of his platoon, ensuring that everybody had been relieved. The smell of wood-smoke from the cooking fires was another pleasant feature of the early morning.

When he returned to his billet, the company commander was there, talking to Koos, with Innocent, as usual, hovering in the background. Captain Jacques was a fairly recent addition to their number, replacing Captain Longwood who had been invalided out with particularly severe malaria.

"We're on the move, Humphrey," he said. "One of the locals apparently says there is a small German detachment encamped a few miles ahead."

"Do you think he's telling the truth?" There had been several instances of information being provided about enemy troop movements which had proven to be imaginary, doubtless intended by their providers to encourage the British to keep on going and not remain as a burden on the local community.

"Who knows? Anyway, the word from above is that we must follow it up, so get your lads together. We need to move out in twenty minutes."

One of the advantages of having very few possessions is that it does not take you long to gather them up for a speedy departure, and Humphrey and his soldiers were ready to move well before the deadline, fires extinguished, and kit packed up. The company, and indeed the whole battalion, had no artillery, but they did have several machine guns and two of the new Stokes mortars which would be useful if they needed to attack entrenched positions.

At the appointed time they set off, first of all in the thick bush along paths and game trails where the need to walk in single file exposed them to the risk of ambush from the flanks. The captain led the way with an African man clad only in a ragged shirt and loin-cloth. This was presumably their informant, which Humphrey found reassuring. The man was surely less likely to lead them to a long-vacated camp or, worse, into an ambush if he was himself in the vanguard. As they emerged onto the more open grassland, they were able to fan out in open order. They walked on cautiously in this manner for, Humphrey judged, something over an hour when the captain signaled them to stop and get down and for Humphrey to come forward. Humphrey worked his way to where Captain Jacques was crouched in the grass with the guide. About a quarter of a mile in front of them was a belt of trees with a small hill rising from it.

"This chap reckons the German camp is the other side of that hill," said the captain, speaking in a low voice. "Luckily he speaks a bit of Swahili." Over the past few months, most of the regiment, including Humphrey himself, had acquired a working knowledge of this widely-spoken language.

The Captain went on. "I think it'd be hopeless trying to attack from the front. There's no cover and they'll see us straightaway if they haven't already. I haven't been able to spot any movement on that hill, but I bet they're there. I'd have sentries up there if it were me. We'll set up the two mortars here with one of the MG's. Your platoon stay with them and the rest of us will circle round as quickly as we can so that we can come in from the left and the right. As soon as you hear sounds of gun-fire, the mortars must lay down rapid fire to land just the other side of the hill, and the MG can spray the top of it, especially if they see anyone running around there. Keep on firing until you see a red flare. I'll put that up as soon as I can see that we're about to enter their position." He grinned. "Don't want to get blown up by our own bombs! As soon as you see that, mortars and MG cease fire and your chaps can charge forward to the hill. I would hope that by that time the enemy will have enough to do without worrying about you. All understood?"

"Yes, sir," said Humphrey.

"Good man! Alright, we'll get on our way. I think this chap can stay with you." He turned to the guide. "We-we simama hapa."

"Ndio, bwana," replied the African with a nod. He looked, Humphrey thought, surprisingly unafraid, and Humphrey noticed for the first time that he was carrying the ubiquitous panga, doubtless as an aid to bush clearing. Humphrey then called in Koos, Innocent, and the other section leaders and explained the plan. Koos sited the machine gun while Humphrey arranged for the two mortar teams to set up their weapons. There was very little cover beyond small thorn bushes. One could only hope that the enemy would not notice them until it was too late. They then all lay down in the grass to wait.

As was his wont when he had time spare for thought, Humphrey let his mind drift back to that extraordinary day several months previously when he had received the letter. He had recognized Oliver's writing on the envelope and had torn it open eagerly to read this rare missive from his elder brother. And indeed there was a letter from Oliver, characteristically brief and to the point, saying that he had been severely wounded, was now recovering well at home, but was unlikely to see active service again. But there was another letter in the same envelope, and as soon as he opened it, he realized who it was from. Ruth! He read it hungrily, hardly believing what it said. Then he read it again, more slowly, still scarcely able to grasp what it was telling him. Two astonishing facts stood out. He was a father! He had a little girl! He did some mental arithmetic and worked out that she must be over two years old now. Why, she would probably be walking, perhaps even saying her first words! And the other was that his fears about Ruth were quite groundless. She had not forgotten him! She still loved him. She was waiting and would be there when he returned! All of a sudden he had the clearest remembrance of her, the last time he had seen her. As she had promised, she had not joined the farewell committee on the railway platform when he boarded the train to

York that early summer morning. As the train drew out of the station, though, he saw her, standing by the road crossing just outside the station, scanning the faces at the windows as the train went slowly by. In an instant he pulled down the sash window, thrust his head out and called her name.

"Ruth!"

Her eyes met his and her hands came together under her chin as though in prayer. Neither had said a word, but they gazed steadfastly into each other's eyes until the train curved round a bend and she was lost to his view.

He could not keep these amazing facts to himself: they had to be shared with somebody and he had sought out Koos and told him the news. Koos had been most satisfactorily impressed.

"Man! That is wonderlike! You have a baba! A dogter! Well done, man!" he shook him warmly by the hand.

"Will you marry her, your girl? When you return home!"

"Koos, you can bet your life on it! And you, you will be my best man!"

This was apparently a concept foreign to Koos, but he took it for the compliment it certainly was and shook Humphrey by the hand again. While this was going on, Corporal Mpika happened by and naturally enquired about the source of his superior officers' joy, so the tidings were shared with him too. As the only survivors in the unit of what Koos had christened rather grandly 'the Malangali patrol' – Ndlovu sadly had died of his injuries and Mpango had contracted typhoid fever a month or two later and had to be repatriated – the three men had a bond that transcended their ranks and the differences in their backgrounds. Humphrey had observed with some amusement the conflict within Koos between his natural indoctrinated bigotry and his recognition of Innocent as a fellow warrior, to whom he owed his freedom if not his life. Mpika was clearly more than just a 'good kaffir'.

Humphrey was roused from his reverie by Koos crouching beside him.

"What do you think is happening? Shouldn't we have heard

something by now?"

"I don't know. They must be taking a long time to get into position. The fact that we haven't heard anything must be good. Unless it means that the Germans slunk off before we got here."

As it happened, they did not have much longer to wait. There was suddenly a furious outbreak of gunfire from the direction of the hill. Humphrey ordered the mortars and the Lewis gun to fire and within seconds mortar bombs were on their deadly way and the crest of the hill was being laced with a deadly shower of bullets. Looking through his field glasses, Humphrey could see no sign of life on the hill itself. The rattle of small-arms fire continued for several minutes. Then a red flare curved slowly up into the air from the trees to the left of the hill.

"Cease fire!" shouted Humphrey and the guns fell silent. "All right, men. Let's go!" And he stood up and led the charge. As he ran on through the grass he was amazed to see, out of the corner of his eye, their guide sprinting on ahead, his panga in his hand.

"Simama! Stop!" Humphrey shouted, but the man ran on, shouting and brandishing his panga. He obviously had a personal interest in the conflict.

As they ran on with no incoming fire, Humphrey began to feel they would get there unscathed. A bare hundred yards from the edge of the trees, he suddenly put his foot in an unseen depression hidden in the grass and fell headlong at the same time as he heard the deadly chatter of a German Maxim machine-gun. As he lay there stunned, he realized that he had, quite fortuitously, happened on a channel across the veldt, probably cut by water during the rains but now dry and concealed by the long grass that had grown over it. The machine-gun rattled again and then again and he heard cries of pain.

"Koos!" he shouted.

"I'm here," came the answer over to his right. "There's a bit of a donga here and I'm in it!"

"So am I! Bit of luck! Do you know what casualties we have?"

"A few. There's no cover. That blerry machine-gun is in the

172

bushes to our front. The mad kaffir out in front went down in the first burst."

"Right. Well, when he next opens up, as long as it's not going over you, we'll jump up and get him!"

"Ja!"

A few seconds later, the Maxim began stuttering. Humphrey sprang to his feet and, out of the corner of his eye, could see Koos doing the same. From the trees in front a wisp of smoke betrayed the position of the machine gun and they both loosed off two rounds rapid fire. The gun fell silent. He glimpsed movement to his left and saw Mpika running forward to where their guide lay motionless in the grass. As he got there, the machine-gun stuttered again and Innocent went down. He also flung himself to the ground and could see out of the corner of his eye Koos doing the same. The Maxim fired some further bursts.

"Koos, I'm going out to get him. Give me some cover."

"Don't be a fool! You can't do anything! At this range they cannot miss!"

"I'm going! When I shout, give me cover. We know where he is now." He gathered himself, gave a loud cry, sprang to his feet and ran forward to where Innocent and the guide were lying. Behind him he could hear Koos' rifle sending round after round. Just as he reached the two men he felt himself be struck on the body in several places and was hurled to the dirt on his back. He heard a loud shout.

"Verdoem bastards!" To his amazement he could see Koos walking steadily towards them, firing his rifle at every stride. The machine gun fell silent again. When Koos got to them, he crouched down beside Humphrey.

"Man, are you alright? Where are you hit?" Humphrey tried to answer but only managed a gurgle. At that point he heard a single shot and Koos was thrown backwards and out of his line of sight. He could do nothing but lie there. He felt no pain, just an increasing constriction in his chest. In his breast pocket he kept a photograph included in one of Ruth's most recent letters. It was taken in a studio in York and showed Ruth and Elizabeth posing rather seriously. It was his dearest possession. He very much hoped it had not been torn or stained. This was his last thought as he drifted into blackness, though he was aware as he did of a burst of gunfire from in front of him. This no longer seemed to matter. Peace was his.

CORRESPONDENCE – 6

Mrs Louisa Nayland
The Vicarage
Cowdenhall
Yorkshire

April 1918

My dear Mrs Nayland

I am writing, as you may imagine, in connection with the terrible news about Humphrey which I know you will have received not too long ago. As a commanding officer I have had to write many letters like this over the past couple of years, but none as difficult nor as heartfelt as this one.

In the months we served together in the BSAP, I came to know Humphrey well, and though our paths have only crossed occasionally since he transferred to the Native Regiment, I have not seen or heard anything to alter my opinion of him.

Humphrey represented the very best our country can produce – honest, decent, hard-working and loyal. You can feel very proud of him and all that he stood for. I have had an opportunity to speak to both of his COs in the RNR and was not all surprised to learn from them of the very high regard and affection in which he was held by all his fellow-officers and the men in his unit. Indeed it would seem that, at the moment of his tragic death, he was engaged in a life-saving effort with two of his closest pals, though who was trying to save whom is not clear. Unfortunately both of them – Sergeant van Rensburg and a very fine African soldier, Corporal Mpika – also perished. I dare say he may have mentioned them to you in the past?

I know there is little I can say to you and the Vicar that will lessen the pain of his loss. Perhaps it will provide some comfort in the future to know that your son was the sort of man that anybody would be proud to call their friend, and those, like me, who did so will always hold him very dear in their memory.

If you are able to do so, I would be most grateful if you would extend my condolences to Ruth and her little daughter. I have not, of course, met them, but the last time I saw Humphrey he was full of their news. His delight in having become a father, really without intent or initial realisation, was wonderful to see, and he lived for the day when they could be together. I can well imagine the misery that Ruth must be enduring.

Please thank Oliver for his letter which, as always, I enjoyed. He does, however, give very little news about how he is coping with the demands of his changed circumstances – the new leg and everything. I would like to know about that! I'll respond to his letter very soon.

We have been watching with intense interest the progress of the war in France and there were certainly some moments of anxiety in the past month or so. From all that we hear, though, the Hun has run out of steam and now that the Americans are there in force it will only be a matter of time before he has to give in. For our part, we have still not managed to catch up with that slippery customer Lettow-Vorbeck – every time we think we have him pinned down, he has wriggled away. Still, his luck cannot last forever and in any case, I suppose that if Germany does capitulate, he will have to give up as well.

Once this terrible war is over, I do plan to make another visit back to the Old Country, so tell Molly not to do anything rash until then, because I will have her lobola with me! I am only half joking about that. If there's one thing I have learned over the past four years, it is that one must realise the truly important things in life and act accordingly.

Once again I offer to you and Rev Nayland my deepest and most sincere sympathy and condolences on your grievous loss.

Yours very sincerely

Marcus Graythorpe (Major)
BSAP
On active service in Portuguese East Africa

EPILOGUE

THE GRAVES

Mathew arose from where he had been kneeling in front of the gravestones. As he stood there he suddenly heard a noise behind him and whirled around. Standing a short distance away was a young African lad. He looked about 18 and was neatly dressed in a white shirt and khaki shorts. Mathew had a couple of times in his walk from the car had a feeling he was being followed and had once turned about without seeing anybody. It seemed his feeling had not been mistaken.

The young man said something in a language completely unknown to Mathew. Mathew shook his head to indicate he had not understood. He pointed, first to himself, then to the middle gravestone, and then once more to himself. The boy came nearer and peered at the inscription, still legible after all these years. 'Lieut H.G.Nayland   Rhodesia Native Regiment 4th March 1918'. He said something that sounded interrogative in his own tongue and pointed to the gravestone and again at Mathew. Mathew felt it was safe to nod.

"Yes. He was my great-grandfather!"

The boy placed his hand on his own chest and pointed at the granite rock next to the three headstones and said something in his language. It suddenly occurred to Mathew that the rock also marked a grave, one without any inscription. Could it be that it belonged to one of this lad's forbears? Was he the one who had been looking after the graves? Mathew made a gesture of weeding and digging around the graves and pointed to the boy with his eyebrows raised. The boy nodded emphatically and patted himself again on his chest. On an impulse Mathew reached forward and shook the lad by the hand. He was obviously somewhat disconcerted by this: his handshake was limp and unenthusiastic, but he smiled warmly and nodded again.

Mathew recovered his camera and took several pictures of the headstones, the graveyard, and the surrounding bushland. He knew it was not at all likely he would be coming back here. He hoped the pictures would enable all three names to be read – Lieut Nayland, Sgt. K. van Rensburg, Cpl I.Mpika, all Rhodesia Native Regiment, all died 4th March 1918.

Mathew was able to persuade the boy to be photographed next to the graves and was entertained by his delight when he was able to show him the result in the display panel on the back of the camera. With the use of involved sign language, he was even able to get the lad to take a photograph of him beside the headstones.

By the time they had completed their photographic endeavours, Mathew glanced at his watch and was concerned to see that it was past four o'clock. If he was to get back to the main road before dark he would need to start making his way back. He gestured this to the lad who looked enquiringly at him and imitated a steering-wheel. Mathew nodded.

"Yes. I must get back to my car." The boy turned and waved for Mathew to follow him. They made good progress and arrived back at the Toyota in little over half an hour, with Mathew more than somewhat out of breath. To his great relief the car seemed untouched. He pointed down the road and to the boy and said, "Chokwe?" The lad shook his head and pointed to another track leading up the donga bank that Mathew had not previously noticed. Mathew nodded and then pointed to himself and said "me, Mathew, Mathew!" He pointed interrogatively at the young man. The boy smiled and said, "Antonio!"

"Thank you, Antonio! Obrigado!" The boy smiled again and then turned and made off down the path which presumably led to his home.

Mathew got back in the car (the remote control still worked!) and started the engine immediately, partly to satisfy himself that it would start, and partly to get the cooling effect of the air-conditioner. Before he set off though, he sat there for a few minutes, getting his breath back and reflecting on one of the most extraordinary days of his life. It had been the culmination of months of investigation and planning, but nothing could have prepared him for the final result of his quest.

He'd hardly known his great-grandmother. He'd been a very small boy when she died. His only memory of her had been of a rather remote and forbidding person with a strong Yorkshire accent. He understood that her husband had died in the First World War. She had never married again. His grandmother, Elizabeth Miller, was quite another matter. She was a happy, gregarious person who took a keen interest in his father and all her other children and their families. She was quite an old lady when Mathew came along, but, as she lived to a very great age, he had plenty of opportunity to get to know and enjoy the love and generosity she took delight in spreading around. Some of his happiest childhood memories were of holidays spent with Granny at her little house in Wetherby and the special treats she would organise for him and his younger sister Caroline.

"Don't tell Mum," she would whisper, "she might not approve."

He had been heartbroken when she had died, just months short of attaining the three figures that would have earned her a telegram from the Queen. He had been only too happy to shoulder the considerable burden of sorting through her personal effects which were very voluminous: Granny Elizabeth was a hoarder! He could not have known what he would uncover, mementoes, photographs, letters, not only hers but her mother's. An insight into a world he barely knew existed. He became obsessed with following the stories they hinted at and which, with the aid of the internet, he was able to pursue. Perhaps not the last, but the remotest, link in the chains was this abandoned little graveyard he had located in rural Mozambique. He knew he had to go there.

Getting there did pose some problems. He had tentatively made the suggestion to his wife, Rosie, that they should go together. Bless her, she had quashed that idea with her usual common sense.

"We can't afford it, Mat, and anyway, you don't need me there. You go. I'll stay and look after the children. We'll be fine!"

And so he'd gone and here he was.

He was still quite shaken by the emotion of the day, but had also a great sense of satisfaction. He felt he had joined a circle that had been left incomplete for nearly 100 years. By finding and honouring the last resting place of the great-grandfather he had, until very recently, been quite unaware of, he had perhaps brought peace to the grandmother he had adored and her mother whom he had hardly known but with whom he now felt such a strong kinship.

He put the car into gear and moved off. As he did so, a dik-dik burst out from the bush beside the path and danced along the road in front of him. About 20 yards in front of the vehicle, the little buck stopped and glanced over its shoulder at him before darting off into the bush at the side. Mathew drove on. He felt very much at peace.

ABOUT THE AUTHOR

Chris Durrant was born in India to British parents in the last days of the Raj. He was brought up in Kenya, had three enjoyable and not completely wasted years at Oxford, and went back to East Africa to work for the Commonwealth Development Corporation (CDC), a sort of British equivalent of the World Bank. After postings with CDC in Swaziland and Jamaica, he migrated with his family to Australia. He now lives with his wife Shirley in the hills above Perth, Western Australia. Children and grandchildren are scattered around the world, including Perth.

Apart from financial management, Chris has worked as a pig farmer and a school-teacher. He is a rugby fanatic, an environmentalist, and a keen student of the history of the Great War, in which his father served and two of his uncles died. He has written his autobiography and a collection of whimsical essays about the school where he worked, as well as numerous songs and comic poems over the years. He has also co-authored several school accounting text-books. *Under the Same Moon* is his first novel.

Follow the author at www.chrisdurrant.com

Printed in Great Britain
by Amazon